What people are saying . . . .

"As an influential thought leader in the field of Analytics and Data Science, Bill has always had the gift of taking complex concepts and explaining them in a manner that allows the rest of us to understand what's going on. In this book, Bill has extended his talent to another, far more important domain—parenting. With every chapter, Bill has taken concepts that can be daunting for parents to articulate to their children—like integrity, trust, confidence—and created a framework that any parent would find valuable to guide those conversations with their own children."

— Jennifer Lewis Priestley, Ph.D.
Professor of Statistics and mother of two

"While there are many challenges in raising and guiding our kids today, open communication with them is probably the greatest challenge that we face as parents. As a parent of two kids, the ideas found in Bill Franks' book are amazingly simple and easy to use. Each chapter offers a great communication starter which you can follow or customize for your own family's needs. The goal is to talk with your child and this book provides an outstanding outline to use."

— Bill Wendell, 6th Degree Black Belt
Owner of Marietta Martial Arts
29 years teaching kids martial arts

"I will be using many of the themes and stories from Bill Franks' book, I Need To Tell You Something, for the weekly Scoutmaster's Moment that I share with my Boy Scout Troop each week. It is common sense and good old fashioned morals expressed in short, engaging and fun to read chapters. At times I felt like the author was reading my mind and writing my very thoughts!"

— Harry Colley
Scoutmaster and father of two sons

I Need To Tell You Something

Life lessons from a father for his teenage children

Bill Franks

Fields Pond Publishing
Marietta, Georgia

Fields Pond Publishing
5052 Fields Pond Cove
Marietta, GA 30068
www.INeedToTellYouSomethingBook.com

ISBN 978-0-9988861-0-7 paperback
ISBN 978-0-9988861-2-1 hardcover
ISBN 978-0-9988861-1-4 eBook

Design: Julie Murkette
Cover photo: ©Photographerlondon | dreamstime.com

Publisher's Cataloging-In-Publication Data
(Prepared by The Donohue Group, Inc.)

Names: Franks, Bill, 1968-
Title: I need to tell you something : life lessons from a father for his teenage children / Bill Franks.
Description: Marietta, Georgia : Fields Pond Publishing, [2017]
Identifiers: ISBN 978-0-9988861-0-7 (print) |
    ISBN 978-0-9988861-1-4 (ebook)
Subjects: LCSH: Teenagers—Conduct of life. |
    Teenagers—Life skills guides.
Classification: LCC BJ1661 .F73 2017 (print) | LCC BJ1661 (ebook) |
    DDC 158.0835—dc23

Printed in the United States of America

Dedication

*This book is dedicated to my wonderful children,
Jesse and Danielle.*

*This is one case where it is literally true
that if it weren't for the two of you,
this book would not have been written.
I hope that as you get older,
you'll appreciate what I have to say in this book.
I really do believe that your life will be better
if you follow my advice.*

*Jesse and Danielle, this time I need to tell **YOU** something!
So, please listen up.*

*Special thanks to Robert Hockett for his initial suggestion
that I write this book and his encouragement along the way.*

Contents

Part One | Maintaining Perspective

Part Two | Making Good Decisions

Part 3 | Setting Priorities

Part 4 | Resisting Pressure and Overcoming Adversity

Part 5 | Keeping an Eye on the Future

Foreword

With our plugged-in, time-starved, and immediate-response world, we are at real risk of overlooking and neglecting the lasting connections that actually matter . . . those in our families. With the sheer volume of work, email, commitments and Facebook posts, it is often hard to find things of lasting value and meaning. Principles held dear, personal beliefs with meaning, and the transmission of true character and integrity to the next generation — and the next — is worthy of our best efforts.

Bill Franks has taken his typical thorough and thoughtful approach to life and applied it to some of the most important topics of conversation we can have with our families — life and success, discouragement and failure, education, honesty and patriotism, kindness and change, money and perspective, decisions and boundaries, and many others — and put them all in a book that is, simply, worth reading.

With an unexpected tenderness and vulnerability, Bill uses personal successes and failures to teach, to instruct and, most importantly, to cause us to "pause and consider."

"Consider what?" one might ask.

"How we share hard-won knowledge, experience, and insight with the next generation," is my answer. Mostly gone are the days of family dinners, abundance of quiet family time and, with them, opportunities to actually connect and share experiences. We all remember meaningful brief discussions, unique events, and shared experiences that occurred during our youth and young adulthood. Some of these experiences affected us and changed our lives forever. This book is a way to proactively, in small bite-sized pieces, have those same brief, but important, discussions and experiences with those we care about.

This book provides us the opportunity to systematically review or just sample a topic in 2- to 3-page bite-sized pieces. Most importantly, the topics are insightful, with concrete examples.

In my experience, meaningful experiences happen in very small groups, individually, or in families. While reading the book, I thought about my own experiences — successes and failures — and the personal examples I will use with my own children and grandchildren.

This is a book that deserves attention. It deserves to be read and discussed with our children and grandchildren. I am looking forward to sharing it with my 12 children and soon to be 11 grandchildren. I firmly believe it can help them to reflect on life, character, and what kind of people they will eventually choose to become.

— Robert Hockett, CFP
Principal/Wealth Manager, Modera Wealth Management

Note from the Author

The title of this book comes from a phrase that my son Jesse first invented and then, unfortunately, my daughter Danielle picked up by watching Jesse in action. It started when they were each about four years old. Whenever one of them was having a tantrum about something, he or she would say over and over, "I need to tell you something! I need to tell you something!" When we'd humor them and ask what they needed to say, it was usually something along the lines of wanting to not be in trouble anymore or wanting to earn back the privilege that was lost. Sometimes they'd cry and scream, "I need to tell you something!" dozens of times. As a result, I thought it would be appropriate to title this book in honor of that phrase.

How this Book Came to Be

In 2009, I began working with a new financial advisor. As we worked through various insurance, retirement planning, and estate planning processes, he had one suggestion that caught me off guard and that I had not thought of. He suggested that my wife and I write a "Statement of Values." I asked him what that was, and he said it was a document where we would outline views on life that we would want to pass on to our children in the event that we died early and unexpectedly.

The idea seemed a bit morbid, but after some consideration, I decided that it was a good idea. After all, what if I did die? What lessons that I planned to teach them as they grew would my children miss? What things would I not have a chance to tell them? If I didn't write it down, they would never know.

After more thought on the subject, I realized that a few-page letter just wouldn't do it for me. I had a lot to say on a lot of topics and it was going to take more. In fact, it occurred to me that I would have a book when I was done writing it all down. As a result, I decided to write that book!

Originally, my plan was simply to self-publish a handful of high quality, leather-bound copies for my children and close relatives. When I was in the middle of writing the book, however, I went through the process of writing and publishing my first business book, *Taming the Big Data Tidal Wave*, with John Wiley & Sons, Inc. Based on that experience, I decided perhaps many other parents would like to tell their children the same things that I wanted to tell my children. The result is what you see here.

Who Should Read this Book

The book is first and foremost intended for my children. I plan to give it to them once they are in junior high school. While the book is a good refresher for adults, too, I believe that the highest impact of the material will be achieved for those in the 12 to 22-year-old range. At that stage, adolescents and young adults are still forming their own value systems and are still struggling with who they will be. The more guidance and support that they get, the better their chances in life will be.

My plan is to read the book with my children. Set aside 20 to 30 minutes and select a chapter. Take a few minutes to each read the chapter and then a few minutes to each think quietly about what you've read. After reading and thinking about each chapter, it should be followed by some meaningful parent/child discussion on the topic presented in the chapter. The discussion will offer an opportunity for parents to reinforce the lesson, put their own twist on the topic, and identify areas where their children may need some gentler parental guidance. The chapters are very short so that limited time is required to read any given chapter. This will help keep young minds focused and engaged. It will allow older children to take it point by point during active lives.

Its Value and Purpose

This book is meant to provide life guidance with the opportunity to apply lessons widely across cultures and religions. Children have opportunities to learn about their religion from other sources, so this book doesn't deal with that aspect of many children's lives.

I have also attempted to avoid politically charged topics whenever possible. As a father, I think that there are some important thoughts on politics for my children to learn from me. I have plenty of time to gets those thoughts across elsewhere and have tried not to focus on political points in the book. Perhaps my political leanings will come through somewhat in the way I present the content. However, I do hope that the way I present it will be found positive and acceptable to those of all political persuasions.

I do not claim that the book is the ultimate authority on how to lead a good life, how to deal with challenges, or how to raise children. The book simply contains my views that I hope my children choose to follow. Any given parent may differ with me on any given point. Parents can consider the content here as a starting point and a way to begin a dialogue with their own children. Any of the messages can be fine-tuned as readers desire to make it their own.

The Format of the Chapters

Each chapter focuses on a single life lesson. Chapters start with an explanation of the core theme of the lesson and why it is important. Then, I provide examples from my life where I have either seen the lesson applied or ignored. Highlighting both failures along with successes bring home the point that living the right way is a constant effort. The fact is that everyone will have some occasions where they act below their own standards. It is necessary to focus daily on making sure those occasions are few and far between. The chapters end with questions that readers can ask themselves as they consider how they will apply the lesson in their own lives.

I have also tried to focus on examples from my teenage and young adult years when possible so that they will resonate better with the intended readers. Soccer was a big part of my life for so many years. As I wrote this, I realized that I got a lot more than just some sports experience, given that soccer made it into so many examples. I also found the process of figuring out what topics to cover and what examples I would use for each chapter to be a very good exercise for me. I encourage any parent to think through the lessons that would be important to them to pass on to their children even if they don't write it down as I have.

One last comment is that I have made each chapter capable of fully standing on its own. While the chapters are ordered and numbered out of necessity, there is no requirement to read them in order. Any given chapter can be read by itself without issue. The only impact that this fact may have is that at times I provide the same background information in more than one chapter. Given that the chapters are only a few pages each and the background information is minimal, readers shouldn't find this to be a distraction.

— Bill Franks

Part One

Maintaining Perspective

Chapter 1
Respect Versus Popularity

There is a critical distinction that should be made between respect and popularity. Not everyone realizes the importance of it. It also isn't something that is easy to focus on when you are growing up and there are pressures all around you to be "cool" and "popular." I was lucky that I wasn't led too astray by failing to recognize this distinction before I did.

Respect and popularity are not mutually exclusive. However, they are not totally intertwined either. More often than not, people are rated much higher on one of the scales than the other. If you can manage to be popular while remaining true to yourself and have people's respect, that is a great place to be. However, you really need to think through which of the two is more important to you and which will lead you further in life. Then, you should focus on pursuing that path in earnest. I certainly hope you'll choose respect over popularity.

You may wonder how I can say the two aren't the same. You might think that the most popular kids have the most respect, but take a close look around and think about it. Are the most popular kids the same ones that people are willing to trust with a large responsibility? Are the most popular kids the ones you would have confidence in to keep a deep secret you reveal to them? Are the most popular kids the ones people want on their team when academic prowess or teamwork is required? Of course there are cases where the answer is "yes". However, in many more cases, the answer will be a very clear "no."

While there are some lucky people with the combination of both popularity and respect, many popular people really aren't that well respected. Sure, people think they are cool and, of course, kids have a natural tendency to want to hang out and be seen with popular people. However, if your life depended on who you chose to be with, would you pick a popular set of teammates, or would you pick teammates you respected and trusted? I believe that most people would go with the latter. If you think about it, I'll bet you do, too.

I knew a lot of people in high school, college, and throughout my career who everyone loved to hang out with. Everybody knew those people were fun and that you could have a great time if you hung out with them for an evening. However, many of those fun people weren't the "go to" people that would be approached when someone really needed something critical done and done right the first time. Many people are great to have around, but they aren't the people to depend upon when times get tough.

I knew others who were the "go to" people. Maybe they weren't as much fun or as good looking, but everyone knew they could be counted on, they had what it took to succeed, and they would do the right thing. Those people had the respect of others even if they weren't the most popular.

The older you get, the more you'll see popularity as being less important and respect being more important. Over time, people realize that popularity doesn't get the job done, pay the bills, or provide dependability. When you respect someone, however, you can expect to get those things. When I was in junior high, it was possible to be a complete loser in many ways, but if you were officially popular, that's all that mattered. By the time I graduated from high school, there seemed to be more of a balance. Popularity was still overrated, but respectability had crept up to be an important factor, too. As I advance in life, popularity is simply a nice trait to add onto respect. Respect is what people want another person to have. Without the respect of others, you probably won't get far in life.

As you grow up, please focus on being someone who earns respect based on your character, actions, and talents. Popularity, or at least enough popularity to let you get by in life, will likely follow.

A Few Examples from My Past

There were a few times in my life where the distinction between respect and popularity really hit home with me. Growing up, I had a friend that was always great fun. He was always willing to do what it took to make sure people enjoyed themselves when he was around. I greatly enjoyed his company and we had a lot of good times together.

However, this same friend wasn't very dependable. He was often late for things. He would commit to doing something and would either not do it at all, or not do it very well. He frequently did things that crossed the line from silly and entertaining to stupid and reckless. I considered him a very good friend for many years. However, I realized over time that I really didn't have as much respect for him as I did for many of my other friends. I liked him (and still do), but I couldn't depend on him (and still can't). I was happy to meet up to go out for an evening of fun, but I didn't want to depend on him for anything important. I don't say that to be harsh or negative; it is just the simple truth.

At the same time, there were people who I didn't get along with as well. I liked them enough to tolerate them and even be somewhat friendly, but I knew I could count on them to come through. If there was a school project, I wanted them on my team. If I was in a bind and needed something, they were the ones I could call. As I grew up, I began to realize that some of those people were better friends than I had originally thought.

I had some similar experiences in college. I knew many people who were popular and who I liked, but who I had little respect for. There were guys, especially in my fraternity, who were wild, crazy, and fun, but they treated their girlfriends poorly, they didn't take school seriously, and they couldn't be counted on to come through on commitments on a regular basis. I had a great time partying with them, but I never really counted many of them as true friends.

Some of my true friends weren't all that popular, but I respected them and others did as well. I trusted them and I could count on them. I realized that I would much rather be the respected person who isn't too cool than the cool person who isn't well respected.

One time, when I was in my mid-twenties, I ran into someone from my high school soccer team. We had always been friendly and I wouldn't have expected either of us to say anything bad about each other, but we hadn't been overly close either. As we talked, he made a comment that has stuck with me ever since. He said something to the effect of, "Bill, you know I always had tremendous respect for you. I know a lot of the other guys did, too. Thanks a lot for helping me out with my math questions and for shooting straight with me in general. I know you'll be a success."

I did not realize until that moment what a great compliment such a statement could be. It surprised me because I had no idea that this person had such a positive view of me. I wasn't the most popular guy on the team, but I had earned his respect. I think that may be the moment where the difference between popularity and respect really hit home. I decided to put the pursuit of respect over the pursuit of popularity from then on.

In part due to that day, I have always focused on doing and saying what I think is right and not doing or saying something because it will be more popular. Ironically, I think I have become more popular as a result, even as I have garnered more respect. I believe people beyond a very early age truly prefer to associate with someone they can trust and respect. Once you trust and respect someone, it is easy to find things to like about them and for them to become a member of your personal "popular" list.

I don't want you to pursue the wrong goal and set yourself back before you realize your error. When you're young, being popular can seem so very important, but don't blindly pursue popularity to the point where you compromise your ability to earn the respect of others. Always put earning respect over being popular. Following that policy may just lead you to more of both.

Taking Action

- Have you been more focused on popularity or respect? Why?

- Do you know people who have a high level of either popularity or respect, but not both? If you were in a bind, which of the two types of people would you want beside you?

- Think about the actions and traits that have led you to respect others. How you can be more diligent in mimicking those actions and more focused on developing those traits in yourself?

- Do you have friends that you associate with mainly due to their popularity? It's ok to have a few friends you don't deeply respect, but have fun with. Having too many will make it harder to keep your focus on the right behaviors and attitudes. Make adjustments to your mix of friends if needed.

Chapter 2
You Can't Control Everything

If genetics work as usual and my children end up anything like me, they're each going to be a bit of a control freak. I've always liked to control things as much as possible, and have caused myself a lot of stress over the years by trying to keep control of everything. I think it's tied to my analytical nature. However, it really isn't possible to control most things fully. It is also a fact that you may think you are in control of many situations, but you really aren't.

Shortly after my mom died suddenly, I was speaking with the minister of our church. He said something that had an enormous impact on me. He said, "Control is an illusion." I thought about that and realized he was right. Neither my mom nor I could do anything about what happened to her and we couldn't have changed it no matter how hard we tried. We had all sorts of plans for what we'd be doing and we thought we had control of our lives. We didn't.

Even things that seem fully in control can veer totally out of control very quickly through no fault or action of your own. Just think of all the freak accidents that kill people or change their lives every day. The control we appear to maintain is truly an illusion most of the time. We are just lucky that in many cases, things go the way we try to guide them. When nothing horribly unusual happens to knock things off course, we mistakenly credit ourselves for success in controlling things.

Consider all the natural disasters that occur around the world on a regular basis. You can save, plan, and do everything else right to have a nice life, but if a tornado blows through town, you might lose your house, become disabled, and possibly lose loved ones. You really don't have control. This is also true with man-made disasters like war. Throughout history, many people have lost everything they own in the blink of an eye due to unforeseen aggression at the hands of others. War breaks out and suddenly all the plans and hard work that people have put into their lives become instantly worthless.

I admit that I am not the best person to be writing on this topic. I still can't stop myself from trying to assert control over my life and the things around me. While I know logically that it won't always work, I can't stop trying to make it work as best as I can. I don't think it's a bad thing to be diligent and take reasonable actions and precautions to influence things your way. After all, if you don't even try to keep control, you certainly won't use the little influence that you do have the ability to exert. Just don't overdo it. I have often overdone it in my life. In retrospect, I could have had a lot more fun and been a lot more relaxed if I had just let some things go and acknowledged that I really couldn't control them. I should have accepted things as they were and moved on.

An interesting pattern I have recognized over time is that I develop a "grand plan" for exactly how I want something to play out. It might involve my career, moving to a new house, or even dating someone. Invariably, my plan ends up not happening as I had diligently planned and originally expected. However, things usually work out fine, if not very well. I have been sure a certain job was going to work out and it didn't. However, a different job that was unexpected and even better did work out. Had I not pursued the first job, the second may not have happened either.

In this way, my planning helped guide me to a better place. However, it wasn't that I was controlling everything, as much as it was that I put myself into a situation where something positive was able to happen. It was entering a process with an unknown outcome that really made the difference, not my specific plan. Throughout your life, you have to put yourself into positions where good things can happen and great opportunities can present themselves to you. Then, act and take advantage before the opportunity passes. Just don't fool yourself into thinking you are fully in control of the process.

Over time, I have started to become happy when I am sure something is heading in a specific direction. The reason is that I now know that I am almost certainly wrong, based on my history of things never going according to my plan. However, my experience tells me that things are far enough along when I get a feeling of certainty that a resolution is close. It simply won't be the resolution I am expecting!

I now enjoy the mystery and anticipation of seeing how things will actually work as opposed to the grand plan I put in place. I've realized that I don't control everything and have come to terms with it much better than when I was younger. I still have a lot of work to do as of this writing, but I hope you will be able to move through the process faster than I did by recognizing your lack of control and trying to adjust your approach to life earlier.

A Few Examples from My Past

An example of how one of my plans went all wrong was when I was deciding to get married. My girlfriend and I had been dating a while and I thought I should marry her, but I needed to be "sure." I had to find a way to prove that getting married to her was the right decision. I am sure as you read this, the whole idea sounds ridiculous, but I was truly very serious about "proving"

I should marry my girlfriend in a concrete way. After all, how could I have control over my plan for life if I couldn't validate a decision this important?

What was my grand plan, you may be wondering. I had my girlfriend come to the beach for a week of vacation with my parents, my sister, and my brother-in-law. My plan was that by the end of the week, I'd have it all figured out and I'd be able to prove that I should or shouldn't ask her to marry me. I would assess how things were going for the two of us and how she was fitting into the family. I was incredibly stressed going into the vacation with all the pressure of the big decision resting on my head. I told my family about my plan and they all thought I was an idiot (I can't argue with that assessment), but I was certain that I could figure it all out with a concentrated effort that week. Naturally, my girlfriend had no idea of my plan and the pressure she was under!

How did it play out? Well, obviously I married her, but not because of that week in the way I had planned. At the end of the week, I still hadn't been able to prove it was the right decision. I couldn't believe it! I had laid out a perfect plan to lead to the decision and I was so disappointed in my lack of certainty. After all of my efforts, how was it possible that I was still unsure? Did the lack of finality mean that it was the wrong decision?

Then an interesting thing happened. I started to realize that I actually didn't feel a need to prove I should get married as much as I had thought I did. Marrying my girlfriend seemed like the right thing to do and I actually felt like I simply needed to go with my gut. Now, this was a totally unconventional approach for me. I never make big decisions based purely on my gut and instinct. What brought me around to going for it was the fact that even in the absence of a way to prove I should marry my girlfriend, I still wanted to do it. The level of comfort I had, going against my nature in such a big decision, led me to the conclusion that I should do it. While it wasn't proof, I decided that anyone who could make me feel that proof wasn't necessary must be the right one to marry.

Even at the end there, I was still trying to twist the facts into a proof and put myself in control, but I was just fooling myself. My grand plan didn't work out at all as I had planned, but things certainly worked out for the better. Try to lighten up your own obsession for control. There is no need to cause yourself the hassle I caused myself over the years by trying to control things too much. The fact is that control truly is an illusion.

Taking Action

- Was there a time in your life when you thought you had a situation totally under control and then everything went sideways? What caused it? How did you react? How can you react differently next time?

- If you think you're usually in control of your environment, give some thought to all of the things that you clearly don't control that have the ability to derail your illusion of control. It can be a humbling exercise.

- Don't interpret the fact that you don't control everything to mean that you should give up and stop trying. You absolutely have to put yourself into position for opportunities to present themselves. You just can't fool yourself into thinking you're fully in control.

- When an opportunity presents itself to you, do you seize it even if you didn't plan for it? Can you identify times in your life where some unexpected good fortune arose indirectly from your efforts to control your future?

Chapter 3
Money Isn't Everything

People get very caught up with money. Is it nice to have more money than less money? Yes. Was my family lucky enough to have more than many families did? Yes. However, when it comes down to it, money isn't what creates the awesome moments and memories in your life. Sure, money can buy an amazing trip to Europe where you get to see a lot of neat people, places, and things. However, you can also generate great memories by going on an inexpensive trip to a national park or even spending time visiting new places in your own hometown.

Think carefully about the things that have really made you happy over the years. Was it a fancy toy? Or playing with that toy with a friend? Was it going to a fancy restaurant? Or having a nice dinner at home with your family? Was it a nice condo at the beach in and of itself? Or being at the beach with your family and having fun together?

If you really think about the things you enjoy most, the vast majority will actually have little to do with money. It is easy to feel that money is a key part of the equation since many of your memories may involve activities that had a cost. However, the most memorable portions of the activities were probably related to the people you were with and the process of taking part in the activity. It is rare that the cost or value of something is what sticks out as having been the biggest factor in your enjoyment. There are very expensive activities that you can take part in that just wouldn't be much fun by yourself or with a random group of people. -

During vacations, my family tended to stay at nice places when we went to the beach, but the places themselves really didn't matter much. We always had fun playing in the water and swimming in the pool. We went out to dinner a lot on vacation, too. However, if we had less money to spend eating out and instead cooked more at the condo, I don't think it would have mattered to any of us at all. We just went out to eat to be lazy and not worry about cooking on vacation. The real treat was the time together away from our day-to-day setting.

I have always viewed money as more of a game than anything else. While I have been lucky enough to make a very good living, I really don't care about the money directly. It is just fun to collect it and try to substantially increase how much I can get paid and save over time. If I lived in a very poor country where I made far less, I wouldn't notice the difference. I'd still have fun going through the process of maximizing what I could get in that environment. I'm not saying this is necessarily the healthiest attitude towards money, but simply that what, at times, may appear to be my interest in money shouldn't be interpreted as being something it is not.

If disaster strikes and my money is suddenly worthless, I won't be thrilled about it, but I know I'll find a way to survive. Some people literally can't imagine a life without money. It is important for you to keep money in perspective and understand that it isn't the most important thing in life.

I have always enjoyed watching my savings grow and comparing what I save each year to the previous one. My family has always lived well below our means because many of the additional things we could spend our money on really don't add much value to life. We can only use so many TVs. We don't need the fanciest car. We are usually as happy to have a meal at a Chick-Fil-A as at a fancy restaurant. I also know that I need to save to survive in retirement. I don't fool myself for an instant thinking that my happiness in old age will be based on the money I have. I hope the money I saved allows us to easily survive and even enjoy some comforts, but it won't determine our happiness. That is going to be determined by other things.

As you grow up, I suggest that you closely evaluate how you look at money. You will have friends obsessed with it. You will also have pressure to keep up with the spending habits of your friends. Just make sure you're spending in a reasonable manner and that you don't get caught up too much in the superficial and frivolous. It can be a vicious cycle once you start. If you decide material things matter most, you'll continually pursue the next purchase. Instead of enjoying what you have, you'll always worry about what you don't have, especially if someone else you know already has what you don't.

Most importantly, there is a big difference between money and being happy and satisfied with your life. Once you have enough money to feed, shelter, and clothe yourself, more money doesn't inherently make you happier. You need friends, family, and a good outlook on life to be happy. Simply getting more money won't change much if you're generally miserable. Focus on enjoying what you have. Beyond what's required to survive, consider money as nice, but not critical.

A Few Examples from My Past

Once, I made the mistake of taking a job primarily because it would provide a large pay raise and stock options. I had my first "I may have made a mistake" moment on my first day of work! That is not a joke. It really was my first day when I initially had a hint of my error. I didn't connect well with the person I was working for and I really didn't fit into the corporate culture at all. It was not long before I moved on. I was able to get another job that paid the same, but I would have taken a pay cut had I needed to. I just wasn't happy at all with my situation. Yes, I had more money in each paycheck than I previously had, but it wasn't worth it. I have never forgotten that experience and now assess each potential job carefully to make sure the money isn't influencing me more than it should.

When my children were little, we often went on hikes at the national parks near our house. There were several within a few miles of home and they had miles of trails through the woods. I loved to get outside and exercise while spending time with the kids. They also enjoyed spending time together, having snacks by the river, and looking for bugs and other animals. I vividly recall one time that we came across literally thousands of baby toads that had just hatched and were blanketing the entire path. It was hard to walk without stepping on any of them and it was a very cool experience. The toads were everywhere and they were barely the size of a dime. The experience had no cost, but was a lot of fun and created a terrific memory. The kids were so cute and excited by the whole experience.

When I think about my family, the vast majority of what made me happy didn't involve spending money. I always loved reading books to my kids before bed. We had great times playing Tickle Monster and running around the basement. Having meals together is something I enjoyed growing up with my parents and continue to enjoy with my family. Lunches at the pool. Popcorn, soda, and a movie. Hikes at the park. Playing board games. All of those moments have been some of my favorites with my children as they grow up. Even if we lost all our money, I could still do those things with them. It is easy to wonder how people living in utter poverty survive and even seem happy. I think it is because they can still do most of the meaningful things that make me happy, too. You see, it isn't about money at all.

Taking Action

- Make a list of the activities that make you happiest. How many of them are based on money?

- Do you make an effort to keep money in perspective in your life? What can you do to avoid putting too much emphasis on material things?

- Do you know anyone who seems too focused on material things and money? Are they happier as a result?

- Think back to your favorite memories. What was it that really made them special? Was money a major part of it or not?

- If you suddenly had only enough money to feed, house, and clothe yourself, would that be so bad?

Chapter 4
Be Thankful for What You Have

It is important to stop now and then to think about how lucky you are. You have a very good life compared to most people in the world today and an even better life compared to the conditions that were common throughout history. Just a century ago, electricity was fairly new, the car was barely invented, and illness was widespread with few treatment options. You are lucky that you live today with all the comforts, medical care, and security we have. You are lucky that you were born in the United States or another highly developed country where even most of our poorest people live better than the majority of the people in the world. You are lucky that you were born into a family that has been able to live a lifestyle that most people over history could only dream of.

It is very easy to go about your daily business and forget to stop and be thankful. Things that, to us, seem so critical and stressful on any given day aren't nearly as critical and stressful as not knowing where you'll sleep, how you'll eat, or how you can get needed medical care. I openly admit that I have not been diligent in being as thankful as I should be. All too often, I get caught up in the tasks at hand and lose perspective. I hope that you will make an effort to truly stop, acknowledge, and appreciate what you have on a regular basis. It is a good practice, which helps you keep a healthy mindset.

If you look over history, it isn't uncommon for entire countries to lose almost everything in an instant. In recent years, various wars have caused massive loss of life, home, and liberty in parts of the world. The largest example for recent generations was World War II, when millions of people, if they survived, ended up transplanted in a new country with all of their money and possessions left behind. While certainly thankful to be alive, I'm sure that many of them also realized how much more thankful they should have been about what they had before the war. Once what you have is gone, you will quickly come to appreciate what you had. Why not appreciate what you have today while it is safely yours?

The idea of being thankful ties into other topics that I cover elsewhere in this book. For example, the truly valuable things in life aren't money or things. Being healthy, being with family, and enjoying sunny days can be appreciated regardless of how nice your house is or how much money you have in the bank. By taking time to be thankful, you'll appreciate good times as you have them. I think you'll also be able to deal better with bad times. The more things you take time to be thankful for, the more things remain to see you through when some of your blessings are no longer there.

One action that helps keep you focused on being thankful is to make sure you pay attention to, and are aware of, those who aren't as fortunate. Your flu won't seem so bad if you think about what someone goes through with cancer. Your dinner that didn't taste very good won't seem so bad if you imagine what it would be like to have no dinner at all. You don't want to be someone who is spoiled, clueless, and completely absorbed in their own bubble of life. I hope your parents have been able to steer you away from becoming that way, but please make an effort to avoid it on your own as well. Without that effort, it is easy go astray.

A Few Examples from My Past

I remember a time in high school when I got a big lesson in being thankful. I was frustrated at being pulled out of a soccer game for a few minutes by the coach. I was lucky enough to be a starter and I was getting quite a bit of playing time every game. However, I had fallen into the trap of focusing on the minutes I didn't get to play instead of focusing on the minutes that I did get to play.

As my time on the bench went on, I grew increasingly frustrated. While it was probably only ten minutes or so, it seemed like an eternity. Finally, I started complaining to the guy next to me about how frustrated I was that I wasn't getting back in the game. After a couple minutes of my whining, he pointed out to me that he didn't have much sympathy since he hadn't gotten into the game at all. I felt horrible and shut my mouth. As I let myself fume over missing a few minutes of playing time, I totally lost perspective that there were those getting much less. Sure, some players were getting more than me at that moment, but I was getting enough time and should have been thankful for that. Certainly one of the rudest and most insensitive things I could have done was to complain to somebody who was getting even less playing time. Yet I got wrapped up in my own world and did just that. I have never forgotten the way I felt that night when it hit me what I had done.

Another time that I wish I had kept more perspective was when we were moving across town to a new house when my children were both very little. We ended up owning both the new house and our old house for a few stressful months. During that period, we had a series of rainstorms so severe that similar rainfalls occur less than once a century. I believe the rainfall total was an outrageous amount—close to two feet of rain in a week. As a result, we got some water in the basements of both houses. I pretty much flipped out and was a total mess of stress and anger.

I was focused on how upsetting it was to be driving across town to our old house to vacuum up water until late at night in the middle of my heavy travel schedule. It certainly was upsetting and nobody would enjoy it. However, it wasn't the end of the world. I lost track of that fact when I was in the middle of it.

In the end, we were able to clean up all of the water in both houses with a few hours of focused effort. We didn't even have to throw anything away since we got to the water quickly. At our old house, which got hit much worse than the new house, there was less than an inch of water in the basement. In the grand scheme of things, we really didn't have it too bad. We didn't focus on that fact while we cleaned, but we should have. It would have made the process much less negative.

While we didn't have it too bad, some of our neighbors had major damage. An inch of water may be a nuisance and require effort to clean up, but that's nothing compared to some neighbors who had several inches or even feet of water in their homes. That led to ruined carpets, ruined furniture, and other damage. I wish I had kept a better perspective and been thankful that we had such slight damage from the start. By losing perspective, I caused myself a lot more stress and frustration than was truly warranted. It is impossible to go through life without some negative events. When those occur, the better you can keep a thankful mindset, the less painful the events will be and the faster they will seem to pass.

One big event in the United States is our Thanksgiving holiday. This day is specifically set aside to be thankful and focus on the blessings you have. The stature of this holiday, as one of our society's biggest, shows that the benefits of being thankful are widely recognized and valued. It has been that way for generations and will hopefully stay that way for many more. If you can make taking time to be thankful part of your routine, it will only make your life better.

Taking Action

- Do you regularly take time to be thankful for what you have? When was the last time? Take some time right now to be thankful.

- Do you sometimes lose perspective when bad or frustrating events occur? Work to change your reaction the next time.

- Whenever you are upset or stressed about a situation, think about those who have it even worse. It won't make your troubles go away, but it can help you keep them in perspective.

- Have you ever said or done something that you regretted later because it showed a lack of thankfulness?

- Think about the most positive, happiest people you know. Do they tend to dwell on what's wrong or on what is going well? What would happen if you shifted your mindset to be more like them?

Chapter 5
Neither Flaunt Nor Hide Your Talents

Everyone has some skills and talents that set them apart from the average person. It might be a high level of ability in sports, in art, in math, or almost anything else. You need to explore and determine what your special talents are. You may not know as you read this what your special talents are, but I am sure you have some. Everyone does.

The important thing is that you find your talents and then cultivate them. You will enjoy the process of honing your skills and the satisfaction that achieving excellence will bring to you. A critical fact to recognize is that whatever your talent is, it may be something another person is unable to do as well. You don't want to gloat, be boastful, or condescending about your talents. That will just drive people away from you and can make them feel bad about the fact they don't share your abilities.

The best thing to do is simply go about your business quietly and discreetly. Those who want to know more about your skills will ask. If you're truly good at something, you won't need to tell people for them to know. It will be obvious to anyone who sees you in action. We can all tell a talented artist, musician, or athlete when we see them doing their thing. In school or at work, you'll also be able to tell who's great at math, science, writing, or just getting things done in general.

At the same time, you don't want to be embarrassed by your talents and try to hide them. There is a huge difference between actively advertising yourself or bragging and simply doing what you do well quietly and consistently. I've seen people try to hide what they are capable of (such as getting good grades) and it is hard to imagine how that can be a good thing to do. First, you'll never develop your full potential if you try to hide your abilities. Second, people will eventually figure out that you are covering up a deeper level of ability, which negates the effort to cover it up. Last, you aren't being honest and true to yourself if you hide your talents.

It can be a very satisfying and fulfilling process to work on building your talents. The process is a good one for teaching discipline and hard work. It will also lead to skills that you can put to use in life, whether as part of making a living or just a hobby. If you are humble and pursue your talents quietly and earnestly, others will appreciate what you do.

One place where people commonly try to downplay their abilities is at school. Sometimes it isn't considered "cool" to be smart and get good grades. It is much cooler to take a cavalier attitude towards school, get mediocre grades, and be a part of the crowd that doesn't care about education. This is a horrible trap to fall into. The truth is that many kids who appear cool and uncaring about school may actually struggle with it and aren't as able to excel in school as you are. That's ok. What isn't ok is when someone tries to cover up their weakness by acting as if they don't care and are purposely doing poorly. You'd be surprised how many of the kids who act like they don't care are actually putting on a show because they aren't able to do much better and don't want everyone else to know that.

It is equally bad practice not to do well in school intentionally so that you can fit in better. Many smart kids get sucked into this pattern and it is a shame. I challenge you to think of any way that purposely doing worse than you are able in school for an extended period will advance you farther than doing your best. I don't think you should ever hide that you're smart or downplay that fact. Just make sure you don't get too full of yourself and you certainly shouldn't rub it in anyone's face.

One distinction that you must keep in mind when thinking of people's talents is the difference between a lack of intelligence and ignorance. Intelligence is something people have inherently. Ignorance is a lack of knowledge. Most people are reasonably smart. Unfortunately, many don't get the opportunity to get a good education and make full use of their intelligence. The fact that a person doesn't know certain facts or isn't aware of specific cultural protocols does not at all imply that they aren't smart. Often, it is simply a matter of ignorance. They are absolutely smart enough to understand the information you feel they are lacking, but they were never educated about it. Be sure not to assume that having more information than someone makes you smarter. There will certainly be times where you're the one who doesn't know something and you wouldn't want others to think you weren't intelligent as a result, would you?

A Few Examples from My Past

Both my sister and I found ourselves at one point or another trying to hide how well we were doing in high school and college. Luckily, neither of us blew our grades trying to be cool, but we certainly kept our grades and test scores as quiet as possible. Over time, it didn't really work. Honor roll announcements would come out, honorary society memberships would be extended, advanced placement courses would be taken, and college choices would be made. Each of these would reveal information about our capabilities, and our academic capabilities were eventually discovered by our peers.

We both expected some negativity and stigma to be attached to the public recognitions that gave us away, but neither of us really experienced any. As is discussed in other parts of this book, once you get past junior high, 99 percent of people really don't look down on those who do well. They might act as if they do at times, but deep down most will respect those who do well in any endeavor, whether academic or otherwise.

The fact that my sister and I didn't flaunt our grades and achievements doesn't mean that we didn't make a very concerted effort to continue to achieve academic success. People that knew us well were aware of our performance from the start even if others weren't. I recall both in college and in high school various people congratulating me on an academic achievement and telling me that they didn't realize I was doing so well in school. They genuinely were happy for me and seemed to appreciate that I didn't rub it in their faces like some other kids did. You wouldn't want someone doing that to you, so don't do it to others.

From the stories above, you may think that I dodged the temptation to underperform in school completely. This actually isn't the case. In fact, I may owe my mom credit for stopping me from possibly going down a different path through her masterfully executed mental trick. When I was in middle school, I apparently decided that it would be fun to mess around in school and not worry about my grades. According to my mom, I came home with a progress report that had grades well below my normal level. When she asked about it, I acted as though I didn't care and thought it was a perfectly fine set of grades to bring home. She could have argued with me or disciplined me, but she did something else entirely. She knew me well and used my own personality against me.

Knowing how competitive I was, my mom decided to downplay the grades. She said something to the effect of, "I only want you to do your best. If these are the best grades that you are capable of then that is fine with me. I am just surprised that you can't do better than this anymore."

I immediately protested and told her that I was able to do better because I couldn't stand the thought that she'd think the grades were truly all that I could do. She stuck to her plan and told me not to get upset and make excuses. If I was doing my best, that's all that mattered and she loved me no matter what grades I was able to obtain.

Her plan worked. I was so bothered that she'd believe I couldn't do better that I had to prove her wrong. I went back to doing my best in school and never wavered again. I often wonder how far I would have taken my little experiment with bad grades if my mom hadn't handled it as well as she did. It is embarrassing that I was so foolish, but being foolish at times is part of growing up. If I can help you avoid being foolish in this way with this story, I will consider that a success.

One last example is from my first two or three college semesters. I didn't live up to my potential. I didn't purposely do poorly, but I got so caught up in my social life and other activities that I didn't put enough time into my schoolwork. As a result, I got the worst grades of my life. By not keeping focus on my schoolwork, I compromised my performance. I felt bad about it and focused on putting my grades first during my final years of college and also during graduate school. I wouldn't have behaved much differently freshman year if I actually had consciously decided to ignore my grades. The intent to take school lightly wasn't there, but the outcome from my actions was the same. Luckily, I caught myself and made corrections before it was too late.

Taking Action

- Have you ever been tempted to do worse at something than you know you are able to do? Why?

- Have you seen others who fail to live up to their potential? What attitudes seem to have led them to their underperformance?

- Are you careful not to look down on those who don't share your talents? Are you also careful not to be boastful about your talents?

- Do you recognize and keep in mind the difference between intelligence and ignorance when you deal with new people who may have a different background than you do?

- What can you possibly lose if you quietly and consistently do your best at everything?

Chapter 6
Respect Those Who Serve You

One of the hardest and most dangerous jobs anyone can take on is to serve in the military and defend our country in times of need. Even in times of peace, those in the military sacrifice a lot to serve us. Military families often have to move every few years to locations around the world. Often, the person serving has to leave their family for many months at a time. There is nothing easy about it.

You should always have respect for those who are willing to make the sacrifices required to serve in such roles. Without having enough people willing to do it, our country wouldn't be the free and prosperous country that it is. Over the past few centuries, countless men and women have given their lives for our country. They have fended off threats that literally could have ended civilization as we know it. They are true heroes and it is important to keep that in mind.

One group that I have always felt compassion for are combat veterans. Many of them faced situations and saw things that nobody should ever see or experience. In many cases, it really messed up their minds and they have struggled to go back to a normal life after returning home. While there are many uses of tax dollars that I will complain about, supporting veterans isn't one of them. The only reason most of them have any issues at all is because of what happened as part of their job serving the country. The least we can do for their sacrifice is to help them in return.

There are those who dislike the military. Ideally that wouldn't be the case, but it is reality. Some people just aren't comfortable with the idea of using force or being involved in violence of any kind. I do wish, however, that people who dislike the military could separate the military as a concept from the people who serve in it. As with any other career, most military men and women are good, honest people who are simply trying to provide for their families. It just happens that these people also focus on keeping the rest of us safe at the same time.

It isn't easy going through the training and doing the day-to-day jobs that military people must do. It has always seemed wrong to me that there are people in our country who hold such service in contempt as opposed to appreciating it. After all, the person complaining about the military wouldn't have the luxury or the freedom to voice their opinions and complain about the military if it wasn't for what the military did over the years to enable them to do so! There is a phrase, "Hate the game, not the player." In this context, it means that even if you don't like the fact that the country has a military, don't make your dislike personal against those who are part of it.

As you get older, please always be respectful to those in the military. Also please be thankful and grateful for their service. Unless you're in the military yourself, you can't fully understand the work, training, and discipline it takes to do their jobs. Also try to remember those who died in combat to keep us safe. Many children grow up without being able to know their mom or dad because a parent was killed in the line of duty. That's very sad and the ultimate sacrifice.

Note that the same sentiment should also be applied to others who put themselves in harm's way for the benefit of the rest of us. Police officers and firefighters are two good examples. Just think of the danger that police and firefighters put themselves in on a routine basis. It is very disturbing to me how many people are "against" the police. Without the police, we'd have mayhem. There are plenty of careers that provide better pay than what policemen earn with a lot less danger. Yet many people make an explicit choice to do such jobs anyway. The rest of us are better for their choices and we should appreciate them for what they do.

Sometimes you will see a situation where someone in one of these roles violates the trust they've been given. Perhaps a policeman is corrupt or a member of the military does something out of bounds. These are the exceptions. Those who violate the trust we've given them should be dealt with severely, but it is important not to assume the exceptions are the rule. It just happens that the exceptions are what tend to get attention.

A Few Examples from My Past

Once I had kids, my respect for military families went up exponentially. It is one thing to be single and be stationed halfway around the world for 9 to 12 months straight. It is quite another to have a wife or husband and children and do the same. I honestly don't know if I could have handled leaving for so long when my kids were little. This is especially true since we were at war at the time my kids were young and there would be no guarantee I would come home again from the assignments.

If I had been drafted or the country was at risk of collapse if I didn't join the fight, I absolutely would have done what I needed to do. However, I honestly don't know if I had it in me to volunteer and be away from the family for so long unless it was truly necessary. I chose a different career path. That's why I am grateful that others did choose the military. On this front, those who stepped up to serve might be able to look down on me, but there is no way I can look down on them.

We had some neighbors with a nephew in the military during a period of war. He was in his early 20's and was just a huge, muscular, massive guy. He was the exact kind of guy you'd be terrified to see coming at you with weapons drawn. He was deployed to the Middle East and saw quite a bit of battle. He even worked his way onto some elite Special Forces teams. Our Special Forces are among the most selective, toughest, and hardest working groups in the world. For the neighbor's nephew to have made it to those levels proves how good he was.

Unfortunately, he had a very bad landing during a parachute jump in training. It caused some leg injuries that were so severe that he was unable to continue in the service. I felt horrible when I heard the news since he was so excited about his role and so dedicated to his service to our country. He had to come back to the states and go about finding an entirely different path in life. I hope he succeeds. He has earned every opportunity for success.

In my line of work providing consulting around analytics, bad incidents passed by after some stress and excitement. Worst-case scenario: I could be fired if things went very wrong, but I'd still be able to get another job doing what I liked to do. Those who dedicate themselves as members of the military, police, firefighters, or similar jobs can have their entire career and life shattered in an instant. That is a very different set of pressures to live under than what I experienced. It is also a very different set of pressures than what you will experience if you don't go into such a role. Don't ever lose sight of how important those who choose to serve are to society and be sure to respect their sacrifice.

Taking Action

- Do you have any friends or family who serve in a military, police, or firefighter role? Thank them for their service the next time you see them.

- Have you ever taken time to consider and appreciate the sacrifices that others make for you by taking such roles?

- Don't allow people spouting negativity about the military or police to draw you in. Without those who serve us in such roles, we wouldn't have the society we live in and the option to complain wouldn't exist.

- Read some stories from veterans about some of the horrible situations they were faced with. Think about how you would handle those situations. If your respect for them doesn't grow, something is wrong.

Chapter 7
Ask and You Shall Receive

As you go through life, you need to look out for yourself. If you need or want something, you need to go after it. You can't sit and wait for others to give things to you. Often, simply by asking nicely, you can get very positive results. Trust me. You'll be surprised at how well it works.

What I mean by the prior point is that you shouldn't be shy about asking for something. It can't be something crazy like asking for a million dollars, but little things can often be achieved by asking nicely. Sometimes even not so little things can be achieved. Want a better table at a restaurant? Ask. Want a room upgrade at a hotel? Ask. Need some more time to finish a project? Ask. If you don't ask, you can be certain that nothing will happen. Asking is really a zero risk action to take. It is surprising how many people don't think to spend the little bit of energy it takes to ask for something in a nice manner. It is very easy and can provide some terrific results.

Of course, you won't always get what you ask for. In fact, in cases where you are asking for something you know is a long shot, you will be turned down far more than you are not, but at least you tried. Even if you only succeed in getting your request met 10 percent of the time, that is more than the 0 percent you would achieve without asking. It doesn't sound like much, but repeated over many years that 10 percent success rate will really add up.

Also take notice of how often you do things for others simply because they asked. What you agree to will often be something you wouldn't have thought of or volunteered to do if somebody hadn't asked. Once you were asked, however, you had no problem agreeing to the request. I am simply suggesting that you give others the opportunity to agree to help you.

Over the years, I have received many small and not so small things simply by asking. It helps you practice being assertive and doing so in a way that isn't pushy. If you can practice making requests that might not be standard, then you'll get better at it. That skill will come in handy in situations where something that really matters is at stake.

Note that when asking for things, you cannot let it upset you if you are turned down. It will happen. You need to get over it quickly. The bigger your ask, the more likely you'll get turned down. Don't forget that.

A Few Examples from My Past

I have a number of fun examples of applying this principle. We'll start with some fun examples before covering some more substantive examples.

When my son was a baby, we were flying back to Atlanta from Washington, DC. We were using free frequent-flyer tickets that weren't eligible for a first class upgrade. However, I knew that the plane had first class seats available. I took my son, who was looking very cute that day, to the counter and told the man that the baby wanted to see what first class was like. Was there any way he could get an upgrade? The man chuckled and then processed our upgrade. He didn't have to. I knew it, and he knew that I knew it, but by asking in an original way, we got it. I have tried this same request at other times and it didn't work, but the fact it worked once makes it worthwhile to try every chance I have.

One time when I was in college, I was with a group that had traveled to a special summer festival at a marina near Virginia Beach. The local radio station was there broadcasting live. I went to the booth and told them I was from Virginia Tech and that they should put me on the radio. I said that I would tell everyone that this party was worth the trip down to the marina even if people were coming from a distance like me. At first, they just chuckled and politely declined. After some more chatter, they agreed to put me on! They had nothing to lose and needed to have some live interviews anyway. Why not let one be me? The people I was with on the boat were quite shocked when they heard me discussing the party on the radio. This is a totally useless case of asking and receiving, but shows how even silly things can be worth asking for just to see what happens. There was really no reason for the DJs to put me on the radio, but I made it fun for them to do it.

Perhaps my best example of this principle, which also had a very large impact, is from graduate school. I was on a teaching assistantship. I got paid $1,000 per month to teach an undergraduate class and/or grade papers for a professor. I heard about another student getting a special fellowship grant that was made available to her for being a female in the department. A fellowship provided the same $1,000 per month as an assistantship, but required no work. A fellowship is simply free money and is more prestigious (and much harder to come by) than an assistantship.

After learning about the woman's award, I stopped by to talk to the graduate administrator. I asked him to let me know if any fellowships came open that I could apply for. He said there weren't any that he knew of at that time, but he would keep me in mind. Within a few weeks, he called me to his office. He informed me about a new fellowship sponsored by Eastman Kodak (a big company at the time). Kodak wanted to start it the following year. He asked me if I was interested. I said, "Sure, how do I apply?" He said, "You don't need to apply. It is yours if you want it." I couldn't believe it!

In the end, I ended up with a free $1,000 per month my second year and a great resume-builder, too. Had I not planted the seed in the graduate administrator's mind to think of me, there is no guarantee I would have gotten the fellowship. At a minimum, I may have had to actually apply and compete. Asking him to keep an eye out for me was very easy and paid out in a big way. A few of my friends were annoyed at my "luck," but I really don't think it was luck. All of them had the same chance I had to make luck happen by talking to the graduate administrator, but none of them made use of it. Therefore, my name was first in the administrator's mind when the time came.

I will tell you one last story that is underway as I write this. It will either go down as my greatest success in the "ask and you shall receive" game or as one of my more ridiculous requests that at least got considered before being rejected. At work, a public relations firm has been working with us on a few initiatives. I have gotten to know the people pretty well. One night over dinner we were discussing how popular analytics has recently become. I mentioned, half-joking, that there should be a reality TV show about how analytics touch our lives every day, even though most people don't realize it. Wouldn't people like to know more about how airlines manage prices or how search engines optimize their search results? The show would have to keep the topics interesting and the technical details to a minimum, of course. I said that I'd enjoy hosting such a show.

After some conversation, the VP from the agency asked if I was serious. I said I wasn't serious at the time I suggested it because I thought it was an impossible premise. However, I would be very serious if somebody was actually willing to make the show. Next thing you know, they set up a few conversations with their connections. Soon after, I flew out to meet with a studio that makes reality shows. They had an interest in discussing my idea! At that point, it was still a 100-to-1 shot at best. The meeting went very well and they decided to pursue the idea and shoot a sample to take to the networks. We signed a contract that let the studio start pursuing the idea in earnest and the odds rose to 10-to-1 or 15-to-1. The odds will improve with every next step we take.

How crazy is it that by simply suggesting I host a reality show, I was able to get into very serious conversations about it with people who can make it happen? Without asking, I can positively guarantee that nobody would have approached to offer me a show. By the time you read this, you'll know if I pulled the show off or not. Even if I don't, it has been a lot of fun to pursue it and I've beaten huge odds to get this far along the path. Not many people get this far and I'm thankful to have had this chance. It helps keep life interesting to have some unusual things to pursue. Just ask!

(An update on the TV show: the studio was acquired literally one week before our sample shoot. This links directly back to Chapter 2 about not really being in control. The acquiring company wanted to take things in a different direction and the deal fell apart. It's still fun to talk about it, however!)

Taking Action

- Are you shy about asking for things? What can you do to help yourself become more assertive?

- Can you think of examples where someone asked you for something and you complied happily? What would happen if you gave others the chance to do the same thing for you?

- As you start applying this lesson by asking for things more often, make a list that keeps track of things you ask for that you would not have asked for if you were not following this lesson. The successes will motivate you to continue!

- Have you ever been beaten to something because someone else asked before you did? Next time, get there first by asking before anyone else.

Part Two

Making Good Decisions

Chapter 8
Honesty and Integrity

This is one of the most important topics in this book, so please read it carefully. I promise that what you are about to read is right. There is nothing more important to success, to being respected, to getting support when you need it, and to feeling good about yourself than maintaining your honesty and integrity. This seems so obvious that it is odd to be writing about it. However, not understanding this principle will undermine virtually any effort you make in life, personally or professionally. I have seen many people who didn't understand this.

I believe there are no better compliments that someone can make about another person than ones like these:

- "He is an honest person."

- "She always comes through on her promises."

- "He has my complete trust and confidence."

- "If you make a deal with her, she'll live up to it."

Having others view you as being honest and having a high level of integrity means that you are doing things right. If you lie, mislead, contradict yourself, don't follow through, or otherwise let people down, then it will catch up with you. In today's connected world, many high profile people have been brought down by a single incident from their past that included a lapse in honesty and integrity.

If people believe you to be honest, they'll treat you better. They'll also look forward to working with you and helping you succeed. Of course, there may be times when you'll be taken advantage of by someone who isn't as honest as you are, but that's life. It will catch up with the other person eventually. You just need to worry about yourself. Don't adopt the "All these other people aren't very honest, so I don't have to be either," attitude. If everyone did that, we'd descend into chaos.

Being honest is often far from the easiest choice. However, just knowing in your own mind that you've played things straight can help you sleep well at night and feel good about yourself. Some dishonest people manage to fool others for a long time, but they are usually found out eventually.

Think about the friends or family you would turn to in a crisis. How many of them lack your trust? How many of them do you not expect to do the right thing? My guess is very few. You might be willing to play sports or go to a movie with someone you didn't think was very honest, but you wouldn't trust them with anything of importance.

What you must do is really quite simple. When given a choice to be honest or not, pick honesty. When given a chance to "practice what you preach," do it. People won't care whether they agree with all your decisions or actions as much as they will care that your decisions are consistent, based on your stated beliefs, and made with good intentions. I have known people that I completely disagree with on virtually everything. I didn't like them and wouldn't live my life in any way like them. In some cases, however, I respected the fact that they were honest about who they were and they lived in a way consistent with that.

A Few Examples from My Past

One of the most vivid memories I have from growing up is of a family vacation. We were entering an amusement park and had to pay for parking. The people working the booth had wads of cash in their hands and weren't ringing up receipts or providing tickets. You simply paid, and were allowed to enter the lot.

At the gate, the attendant gave my dad too much change. Dad told the attendant and returned the money. The attendant seemed shocked. As we pulled in, my sister and I ripped into my dad about why he gave the money back when nobody would know and the attendant didn't even care. His answer was succinct: "There is a fee to park and we owe that fee. The money I got back wasn't ours, it was the park's. Giving it back was the right thing to do."

I've never forgotten that moment. My dad was right and I felt like a jerk for giving him a hard time. I remember that moment when I am faced with similar situations. Several times over the years I have returned extra change when a cashier has made a mistake, just to prove to myself that I was as honest as my dad.

Let's move on to integrity. To me, this means being consistent and standing firm for what you say you believe. For this example, I'll go back to college. I was in a fraternity and we were holding our yearly elections. As part of the process, each person running gave a speech for themselves. Two other members also give a speech on their behalf. The idea was that based on who was willing to speak on your behalf and what they said, people could better determine who was best for the job. We can all make ourselves sound good in a speech, but to get someone else to make us sound good requires them to be sincere.

So what went wrong? A highly respected member also held a major office. Even before this incident, I never had a good vibe about him. However, because I didn't have any tangible reason for my doubts, I kept them to myself. He spoke on behalf of a good friend of mine who was running for an office. Based on who my friend's opponent was, it was clear that my friend was not going to win the election. Despite that, I was pleased that a person others held in high regard was willing to stand up and speak for my friend. He did a great job with his speech.

Then things took an odd turn. The person who had spoken on behalf of my friend was sitting next to me as we wrote down our votes. Before folding his up, he showed some of us that he was voting for my friend's opponent instead of my friend, even though he had just given a strong speech supporting my friend. He shrugged as if it was no big deal, but I couldn't believe it.

That person lost any respect I had for him at that moment. I never trusted him again and stayed clear of him. What a lack of integrity he showed with his behavior. If he didn't want my friend to win, he could have simply said he would not speak on his behalf. People were known to do that. Once he agreed to speak on his behalf, he needed to vote for my friend. He was dishonest to my friend and dishonest to the fraternity. That incident is one of the clearest examples of a lack of integrity that I have ever witnessed. I swore to myself never to do the same.

To bring it full circle, a year later I agreed to speak on someone's behalf for an office. As luck would have it, the only person I would have preferred to that person later entered the race. However, I was friends with the person I agreed to speak for and did not feel right backing out after making a commitment. From the start of the race, it was expected that he would lose by a moderate margin. When the time came, I gave a strong speech on his behalf, even though I didn't think I would be impacting the outcome of the race. I voted for him as well.

The vote was a tie and we had to have a re-vote. At that point, the thought crossed my mind that I could simply switch to the other person who I somewhat preferred, but I quickly pushed it out of my mind and voted for my friend again. At least one person did switch his vote and my friend lost by a very slim margin on the second vote.

At the time, I believed I acted with integrity. However, the right way to handle it would have been to tell my friend I couldn't speak for him once his opponent entered the race. That would have been uncomfortable, but that would have been right.

Instead, I almost got someone elected who wasn't my first choice, just because I didn't want to hurt his feelings by making the hard choice to back out of my planned speech. Had I not spoken for him, I would have voted the other way and his opponent would have won the first vote. I did not act with full integrity even though I showed some integrity at various points in the process.

As you can see, it is not easy to maintain your honesty and integrity. It takes constant diligence and effort; one major lapse and you can be forever branded as someone who lacks honesty and integrity. I've slipped up at times and sure wish I hadn't. Luckily, my lapses have been minor and not publicly visible. I would have slipped up more often and to a lot larger degree if I hadn't been highly focused on trying to do the right thing throughout my life.

Taking Action

- Who are some role models in your life who you believe display solid honesty and integrity? What can you do to be more like them?

- Have you ever had a lapse where you were dishonest or lacked integrity? What led you to the lapse? What can you do to ensure you do better next time?

- What are some examples where you've seen others show a lack of honesty and integrity? How did you feel about them and their actions?

- When you consider those who you respect and trust in life, how many of the individuals do you feel lack honesty and integrity?

- Have you made a commitment to yourself to always do the right thing even it if is difficult or uncomfortable? Without a strong commitment it will be easier to lapse, so make that commitment now.

Chapter 9
Taking Responsibility

One of the most important concepts that can be instilled in you is taking responsibility for yourself, your actions, and your future. Nobody is going to look out for you like you will look out for yourself. If you need something to happen, you need to make sure you lay the groundwork for it to happen. If you have a situation where some bad luck has impacted you, it is up to you to figure out how to get out of the mess and fix it.

Too many people sit around expecting someone else to make things happen or to fix things. Those people are usually very disappointed with how things turn out. Often, they will blame all sorts of people or organizations for the outcome. In fact, most of the time it is their own actions, or lack thereof, that are to blame.

In the early days of the United States, life was rough. People went out into the wilderness with nothing but some horses, some supplies, and their family. To survive, it was necessary to work hard and take care of yourself. There was quite literally nobody else to take care of you. As a result, most Americans were hardy and self-sufficient. Taking handouts or being lazy just wasn't part of the culture. You wouldn't eat if you didn't step up and make sure you had food for yourself.

As the country grew and became more urban and wealthier, social safety nets were put in place. Food stamps, welfare, and childcare assistance are now offered. The amount of "free" money and resources available has risen to a level where people can survive without really doing anything. You can't be successful or make a large contribution to society, but you can survive. In fact, today you can have an apartment, a TV, a phone, and food without working at all. All of the assistance programs were put in place with good intentions. The goal was to help people out during a time when they needed it— until they could get back on their feet— not a replacement for personal responsibility.

As you get older, you'll find that actions taken with good intentions sometimes backfire due to unintended consequences. Because of our assistance programs, entire segments of society have practically dropped off the map, become totally dependent on government handouts, and have lost any semblance of personal responsibility or work ethic. They feel they are "owed" things from the government (which is really their fellow citizens), and simply complain and wait for the government to fix their problems. As a result, they are in a vicious cycle of poverty and dependence that is often passed on to their children.

My intent here isn't an anti-government rant. The point is that the absolute last place you should ever look for help is the government. It is a big, bureaucratic monstrosity. It often has seeds of good intention that have grown into counter-productive and wasteful realities. Once you decide that your life isn't up to you, but that the government (or anyone else) should take care of you, you are done for. Don't ever let that happen. Even a small, non-bureaucratic private charity can allow you to become addicted to its support. Of course, there are exceptions to this—if you are afflicted with an extreme disability, for example. What I am discussing here are the able-bodied people of sound mind who fall into the pattern of not taking care of themselves, not the people who have no choice.

You need to understand and believe that you are responsible for your future. You are the only one, along with your family, that will truly put your best interests first and have a primary concern in helping you succeed. As soon as you start blaming others, you are letting yourself off the hook a little bit at a time. There certainly are times where someone else has done something that impacts you in an unfair and adverse manner. That's life. Accept that you got a bad deal and move on. Take the hand that you hold at the time, figure out how to play it, and turn things around.

Pay attention to your friends at school, as well as people you encounter elsewhere in your life. I can guarantee that the people who take control of their situations will be more successful and more able to handle difficult situations. Watch how a motivated person who takes responsibility steps up to a given task or situation. Compare them to someone who is lazy and always wants outside help. The difference will be as plain as day.

I can't think of anything that exemplifies the successful from the dependent, the motivated from the lazy, and the reliable from the unreliable more than personal responsibility. I hope your parents have helped instill in you the importance of taking personal responsibility at all times. I also hope that you'll ask what you can do to address a given situation before you ask someone else to address it for you.

A Few Examples from My Past

There was a very cheesy reality game show on TV in the early 2000's. I recall a scene that sums up how different outlooks on life perpetuate themselves and almost ensure that outcomes will occur in a certain way. I am still shocked by this story. Not only was it shocking to me how the woman I'll tell you about handled the situation, but also that a number of the other people present supported her viewpoint.

It was a very simple contest. One contestant was going to win a new car by outlasting the others. Whoever sat in the car the longest won the car. I think they had a five-minute bathroom break every hour, but other than that, the game would continue as long as it took. After several hours, there was only one man and one woman left. The other contestants had dropped out because they didn't care enough about the car to go through discomfort for it.

Here is the interesting twist. The male contestant was actually a wealthy businessman who was on the show for the fun of it. He certainly could use the $1 million winner's prize that would go to the season's winner, but he didn't need it. The woman was a poor, single mother who was barely surviving. She desperately needed any money she could get and certainly could have used a new car. You'd expect that the woman would outlast the man because she'd do whatever it took to improve her situation, right? She'd be incredibly motivated to win that car, right? Wrong!

Shortly after it was down to the two of them, she started pleading with the man to let her win because she really needed the car and he did not. He told her that if she needed the car, then she should outlast him in the contest. Eventually, the woman just quit. Her reason was that she knew she wouldn't be able to last longer than the man and she was upset that he was so cold-hearted. Several other contestants also thought the man was being mean simply because he wanted to win the car.

Why is this significant? The attitudes displayed in the game exemplified exactly why the man was wealthy and the woman was poor. The man was willing to push hard and do what it took to win. The woman didn't believe in herself and wasn't even willing to try to win. How did she know she couldn't outlast him? How could she not even try, given how badly she needed the car? I suspect that many of her life decisions and challenges went the same way. She would give a minimal effort, decide the odds were stacked against her, and give up. How could she ever win with that attitude? Worse, neither she nor some of the other contestants were able to see the ridiculous nature of her attitude. She is destined to struggle for the rest of her life due to her lack of personal responsibility. The man will probably continue to achieve success.

I often see personal responsibility in action during group projects, at school and at work. Often, a group of people is on the hook to produce something together. In my experience, one or two members of the group usually do most of the work, while the others do virtually nothing. Is it fair for the non-contributors to get a good grade along with the contributors who did all the work? Not really. However, the only alternative is for the contributors to decide that they won't do more than the others out of a sense of fairness. Choosing that alternative ensures a bad grade for all. Consequently, those who take personal responsibility ensure that they get a good grade and have a successful project. They also help their undeserving teammates get the same grade. It frustrated me every time I did the work and others got the benefit. However, I had to take responsibility for my own grade and helping the slackers was an unfortunate side effect of what I had to do.

Over time, non-contributors will probably continue to fail to take responsibility and contribute in such situations. Eventually, their attitude will catch up with them. When it does, they may even complain. They won't recognize that they had the power to ensure their own success, but failed to take responsibility. It is better to pull a few others across the finish line with you than to not get there at all. You have to trust that your dedication will pay off over time.

Taking Action

- Have you ever found yourself blaming others rather than blaming yourself? Have you ever expected someone else to fix a situation rather than stepping up and fixing it yourself? Why?

- Do you know anyone who doesn't seem to be motivated to take responsibility for their situation and their future? What do you think leads them to have that attitude?

- The next time you find yourself in a bad situation, commit to taking responsibility to make the best of it, rather than sitting around feeling helpless and looking to place blame. Placing blame will change nothing.

- When you find someone else feeling helpless and unsure of what to do, try to help them find a way to take responsibility. A little help may be all it takes to get them back on the right path.

- Can you think of even a single way that not taking responsibility for yourself, your actions, and your future can be beneficial?

Chapter 10
Keeping Your Word

As you grow up, it is critically important that you always keep your word. When you tell someone you'll do something, do it. When you tell someone you'll pay for something, pay for it. When you tell someone that you've made a deal, keep it. One of the most important aspects of your reputation is to be known for keeping your word. People who are known for not keeping their word lose a lot of respect and will have a much harder time socially and professionally. I imagine that it has a big impact on self-respect as well.

A century or two ago, most important matters were settled with a person's word. There were lawyers and contracts, but many people still went with "gentleman's agreements" and a handshake. Of course, there were dishonest people, but it seems people took their word much more seriously than they do today. Even when I was growing up, finding technical legal loopholes to alter a deal after the fact for personal gain was frowned upon. Today, it seems like many people have no issue with any behavior as long as it is technically legal. What isn't considered is what is ethical and honest, versus what is simply legal.

Aim for a very high standard. Just because something is legal doesn't make it right. When you give your word, you should mean it 100 percent of the time. Don't be in a position where anyone can legitimately claim that you backed down on your word. That can derail trust from others for the rest of your life. There will be times that someone reneges on their word to you. In no way does that provide you a one-time pass to get even by doing the same in return.

I believe that we have entered a dangerous spiral where many people accept the premise that if something is legal, then it is ok. As a result, we end up with all sorts of complicated contracts and legalese documents that supposedly protect against someone being dishonest. However, no matter how complex a legal document may be, it will always fail to address something. Worse, the longer and more specific a document is, the easier it is to claim that something not mentioned is fair game. After all, given all the details mentioned, anything important is surely in there, right? As a result, we have hideously complicated and expensive legal processes that are actually making people less likely to keep their word.

When you make a deal, always be very clear with everyone involved about what you will do and do not intend to do. Once you enter into an agreement, meet those guidelines diligently and completely. That is the honest way to live and it will let you feel good about yourself. When you consistently do the right thing, others will take notice as well. It will establish a respectable reputation for you that will give you a better chance for success in whatever you pursue in life. Nobody wants to deal with people who are known for breaking their word.

A Few Examples from My Past

When my children were young, the world went through the major economic recession that started in 2008. Many people, including my family, lost considerable amounts of money from our retirement savings. Many people also lost their jobs. Simultaneously, home prices dropped substantially for the first time in decades and many people lost their homes. With no job and no income, they couldn't make the promised mortgage payments. As a result, the banks foreclosed on their homes and sold them to recoup what equity they could. That is a horrible and humiliating spot to be in and I am thankful that our family was never faced with it.

A mortgage was traditionally viewed as a personal promise to pay a certain amount of money back over time. The ability of the lender to foreclose was only intended to address cases when someone hit on bad times and could no longer, or refused to meet their obligation. Technically, however, a mortgage says that you'll either make your payments or the bank can take your house.

As the crisis went on, some people began taking a non-traditional approach to their mortgages. The argument was that homeowners were still living up to their word if they let the bank have their house and walked away from their mortgage. Perhaps a person was easily able to pay for the house and had a lot of savings. Some people didn't care. They believed that since their houses went down in value, and they didn't want to be stuck with the loss, they would walk away and stick the bank with the loss even though they were perfectly able to pay.

I think this practice is highly unethical and those involved did not keep their word. Technically, it is legal, but the agreement with the lender was made in a totally different spirit. I would never trust, hire, or rely on anyone who walked away from a mortgage in that manner. I respect those who continued paying for a house worth far less than they owed. They had given their word and stuck to it. Be sure you'll be in that group if faced with a similar challenge in your life. Passing off your problems onto someone else isn't an acceptable approach.

Another example is from a book I read that was written by a very successful businessperson. He had a section on the importance he placed on keeping his word even when others around him would try to find any loophole to take advantage of him in complex business contracts such as acquisitions or mergers. He was disappointed that so many of those he dealt with were surprised and even shocked at his dedication to being honest and keeping his word.

One story he told involved an agreement he made to sell a portion of his company to another organization. The CEO of the acquiring company made a deal, and then took many months to finalize the details. As luck would have it, market factors changed in such a way that the division being sold was suddenly worth two or three times more than when the deal was signed. This turned the sale into a bad deal for the current owner. The CEO of the acquiring company assumed that the author would look for any loophole to renege on what had become a horrible deal, so he offered some concessions to try and avoid losing the deal.

The owner turned him down flat and said he'd sell at the agreed upon price. The other CEO was shocked and asked why he'd stick with such a bad deal. The owner responded that he'd stick with it because when he made the deal, he considered it fair. The acquiring CEO had done nothing to take advantage of the situation; it was just bad market timing. To me, the author who shared that story passed the ultimate test of keeping his word. When you would be better off getting out of a deal and you even have a chance to do it, will you stick with your word like he did? While many people would not, I hope that you will.

Another example is from college. One weekend, some students from another school came to town. They were members of another chapter of my fraternity and I had even met one of them previously. He lived down the hall from one of my high school friends at his school. The visitors asked if they could borrow a piece of equipment that cost about $80. I didn't have such an item, but I knew a friend who did and I borrowed it from him. In turn, I lent it to the visitors.

The visitors ended up leaving without returning the equipment. I am not sure if they stole it or just forgot, but in any case, it was gone. I could have tried to back out of paying my friend, since it really wasn't my fault that it was stolen, but that would have been wrong. I had given him my word that I would watch over it and it was lost or stolen on my watch. I paid my friend the $80 and apologized for the hassle he'd have getting a replacement. At the same time, I knew that I would never trust those visitors again. At some point, even if keeping the item had been an accident, they surely noticed that it had not been returned. If they were honest, they would have contacted me and arranged to return it. I never heard from them again.

Taking Action

- Is keeping your word important to you? If you haven't considered it before, vow right now to always keep your word.

- Have you ever had someone go back on their word to you? How did you feel at the time? What did you think of that person as a result?

- When dealing with others, are you sure to follow the spirit and intent of your agreements and not just the precise legal requirements? Don't look for loopholes to exploit.

- If you are part of a group that enters into a deal, do you push the others in the group to stick to the deal? Take a stand when necessary and you may help someone else reevaluate the seriousness with which he or she takes his or her word.

- Once someone has shown themselves to be untrustworthy, avoid any future agreements with them. There are plenty of honest people out there to deal with. Why would you deal with anyone who isn't honest?

Chapter 11
Think About How Your Actions Would Look to Your Parents

When it comes to making good decisions, you won't be perfect. Whether you accidentally make a bad decision or decide to make a bad decision in a moment of weakness, be prepared to face the consequences. If you want to stay on the right path, make the effort to focus on making good decisions every day. It is often much easier to make a bad decision than a good one. It takes effort to ensure you've thought things through and are considering all the facts and consequences. You'll need to make that effort if you're going reach your highest potential.

If you're in a situation where you don't know what to do, there is a simple test you can take in your head to help you decide. Just think for a moment about what your parents would think if they knew what decision you made and why. Would they be proud? Ashamed? Approving? Disappointed? Deep inside, your gut will tell you. If the thought of explaining the details of what you're about to decide to your mom or dad makes you feel uncomfortable inside, reconsider the decision you are making.

This test works because there is nobody who knows you as well as your family, and there is nobody you know better than your family. You know what your family will think about any given issue much better than you know what somebody else will think. If you sense your family wouldn't like something, you're likely right. Stopping to ask the simple question, "What would Mom or Dad think if I explained this decision to them?" is well worth it.

In cases where you genuinely don't know what your parents would think because it is a situation they couldn't relate to, consider someone else—a coach, a teacher, a friend, or a member of the clergy. Just ask yourself what somebody else, who you respect and who has been in a similar situation, would do in your place. It forces you to look at the facts and how your decision will reflect on you from the perspective of others and helps push aside selfish motives.

Worst-case scenario: you don't consider what your mom would think, you do something stupid, and you have to explain it to her later. That can be quite humiliating and embarrassing. You don't want to do that more than you absolutely have to, but it will happen at least a few times in your life. The key is to learn from the experience and make a better decision the next time. Another benefit is that you can remember how horrible you felt explaining what you did to your mom or dad. You won't want to go through it again. This can help you make the right decision the next time.

A Few Examples from My Past

One time I was incredibly tired and had been having a very stressful week. I had to get a long, late flight that wasn't even taking me home, but to another city I had to visit. I was not in a good mood or a good mindset. An older gentleman and his wife were getting settled in the row in front of my seat. I went to put my bag in the bin above their heads and they objected, saying that they had something they were about to put there.

There is no rule on airplanes that provides use of the bin above your head, but it isn't unreasonable for someone to assume if they haven't flown much. Common courtesy and politeness implies I should have immediately deferred to an older couple and found another spot for my bag. I did put my bag elsewhere.

At this point you might think I did the right thing, but moving my bag isn't the only thing I did. I really unloaded on the man and got very nasty. I don't remember my exact words, but I made it quite clear that they were being ridiculous and that I was not happy with the need to move my bag. I didn't curse, but I'm sure I looked like a real jerk to everyone around and especially to the couple. My reaction was extreme for the situation.

I give the couple credit for remaining seated and not responding to me. They were the better people that day. As I sat for a few minutes, what I had done sunk in and I felt very badly. I thought about how I would feel if someone had treated my grandma that way. Worse, I thought about what my mom or grandma would think if they saw a video of the incident. I knew I had made a very bad decision. I leaned forward and apologized profusely. The couple didn't seem to accept the apology, and I don't blame them, but at least I recognized the bad decision I had made. Ever since, I take a deep breath, and try to think before I speak or act when I am stressed and tired. There are often stressful situations involving grumpy people when travelling. Don't let it get the best of you like I did in that instance.

As a teenager and young adult, you'll have many chances to make a fool of yourself and get caught up in bad behavior. It is very easy to just go along and do whatever those around you are doing. Don't underestimate how stupid, inappropriate, or offensive an idea can be when it pops into the head of a young person. When you are with a group and a bad idea is put forth, there are times that the group decides to go with the idea anyway. It might be an idea that none of the group would ever individually pursue, but somehow in the heat of the moment and with peer pressure in abundance, everyone just goes along.

I've been in situations where people have suggested everything from vandalism to bullying, and even theft. In most cases, they weren't bad kids—they were good kids considering a very bad idea. Luckily, the group of friends I hung around with didn't have as many bad ideas as some others, and we tended to reject the ideas, even though sometimes it took effort and some heated discussion. While I wish it wasn't so, we did cross the line a few times.

One night we thought it would be great to bring some bags of sand to the school beach party dance. We decided to grab some bags from the local lawn and garden center, but it was closed when we got there. To avoid foiling our grand plan, a few guys ran up to the pallets of sand, grabbed a few bags, and put them in the back of the pickup truck. We then went on to the dance, happy with our antics, which seemed quite daring and exciting.

It was only later that I thought about it and realized that we had just stolen. That hadn't been our intention. We were just having a good time and wanted some sand, but we let our guard down and made a very bad decision. Had we been caught, we could have been in real trouble. We let ourselves get caught up in the moment and only focused on the fun we were having. If any one of us had asked what our parents would think about us grabbing the sand when the garden center was closed, I suspect we would have gone to the dance without that sand.

Taking Action

- Have you ever done something that you were later embarrassed to admit to your mom or dad? How did the discussion feel when you admitted it?

- Do you take a moment to step back and think before taking action, especially when with a group having fun or when highly stressed? It can pay off to consider what your parents will think of your actions.

- Consider taking a moment to reach out and actually talk with your parents or another trusted individual when you are faced with a decision and you are uncertain how to handle it. Who is on the list of people that you can you talk to?

- Consider discussing the concept of thinking about what your parents will think about decisions with your friends. The more people that are considering it, the better the chance that someone will speak up to push you and your group to a good decision.

Chapter 12
Doing Your Best

Ibelieve in doing your best at whatever you do. I don't mean that when you're playing a game with a child that you have to try to beat them. I also don't mean that at a fun picnic event you have to spike a volleyball every chance you get against people who have never played. What I mean is that when you are doing something meaningful and important, you should do your best. If you aren't willing to put your best effort into something, then you shouldn't do it at all.

I don't believe that much of what I've achieved in life was because I was far better at the required skills than those I competed against. In some cases I was clearly better and, as a result, I won. In other cases, I really don't think I can credit my skill. In many cases I think the big difference was that I did my best and put a strong effort into the task. This included sports, work, parenting, and volunteering, among other things. By trying harder than my opponents, I was able to win even though I might not have had superior skills or raw talent.

If you're really trying your best, people will notice and appreciate it. In addition, if you're up against those who aren't putting in the effort, it really isn't a fair fight and you can win easily. I always look at it from two perspectives. The first is, for my own pride and sense of accomplishment, I want to do my best. I don't like the feeling I had at times when I knew I didn't try my best. It made me feel weak and lazy. The second perspective is more important. I feel I owe it to those depending on me to do my best. They are putting their trust in me to succeed at whatever the task is. It could be winning games with a team, landing more business at work, helping my kids grow and learn, or helping the church raise more money to support itself. In the end, I take seriously the fact that others are counting on me to do my best.

If you are counting on someone to make something happen for you, don't you want to know they are giving it their all? It is that simple. If you want and expect others to give their all for you, you have to do the same for them. In the event that you don't think you'll have the time, energy, and/or passion to give your all to an endeavor, then you should politely decline to accept the challenge. Most of the time, people will appreciate your honesty. Occasionally, someone will ask you to give whatever you can and they will accept the fact that you'll be giving less than your best. In cases that less than your best can make a difference, that is still a good thing. Just make sure everyone understands what you're committing to in terms of effort.

You'll probably have friends and acquaintances who routinely take the easy way out. They may tease you about being too serious and may boast about the easy time they are having while you're working hard. Don't let it influence you. In the long run, you'll be better off for your efforts and their slacking off will eventually catch up with them.

One of the nicest compliments you can receive is someone saying that you always give your best effort. People know it is a rarer trait than it should be and appreciate it when they see it. You'll appreciate it in others as well.

A Few Examples from My Past

I played soccer for many years. At times, I played at a very competitive level, while growing up and in adult leagues. I was not always one of the most skilled players on the team; if the team was made to perform skill drills, I wouldn't have been one of the standout performers. However, I always played hard and stayed in great physical shape. I tried as hard as anyone on the field, and because I pushed myself and played to win, I could compete with players who were inherently better than me. I would exert the extra effort and would still be able to run late in the game when those less dedicated were too tired.

I never had trouble finding a team to play on and became a captain or manager on many teams, even though I wasn't the best player. As they got to know me, people knew I took things seriously and could see that in how I played. I was always frustrated watching highly skilled players who were lazy or indifferent. It drove me crazy, but that's how some people are.

On the other hand, I have turned down requests because I knew that I couldn't do my best to fulfill them. For example, there was a time when our church was having a great deal of difficulty with finances. I had recently been pulled onto the finance committee and was already stretched thinner than I should have been. When the next pledge drive came around, I was asked to organize it. I knew what a big job that was and I knew there was no way I could do it the way it needed to be done.

My work was keeping me on the road and I was working too many hours already. I had a baby and a three-year-old at home. I knew that I wouldn't have the energy required for the pledge drive to be a success. If I tried, I'd end up diverting too much energy from work and family so that my performance on those fronts would suffer. I would feel like I was failing at all of it. As a result, I just said no. I felt the church, as well as my work and family, deserved my best. I couldn't do my best on the pledge drive and I knew it. Fortunately, they found someone with the time to do it right and I never regretted my decision. It was quite awkward and uncomfortable to say no to a request as important as running a pledge drive, but I believe that I made the right choice.

One occasion where I didn't do my best was in high school. I ran winter track so that I could keep in shape for soccer through the off-season and because I loved the exercise. However, many joined the team because track was important to them and the coach took it very seriously. I always thought the coach understood that track was not my highest priority, but I may have been wrong.

Once in my senior year I had to miss a big track meet due to a soccer tournament. The coach was mad at me and disappointed— she thought I should have stuck by the team until the season ended. This was shortly after she had put a junior in place as captain rather than me. Because I was a senior and a four-year member of the team, I was annoyed by the choice of captain. Then I realized that he deserved it. The fact was that he was dedicated to the team and was doing his best and I wasn't. I really didn't deserve to be captain. In retrospect, I am surprised that I was able to realize that at age 18! It just shows you how obvious it was. I would have looked like a real jerk if I had protested the choice of captain.

The coach was clearly aware of my less than total contribution, especially given her wise choice of team captain, but her disappointment over the meet really stuck with me. Winter track wasn't just a fun pastime for her and many others on the team; they were actually depending on me to help them win. I had become one of "those guys" who didn't try my hardest and I wasn't fully dedicated. I probably should have been running on my own instead of being on the team and letting them down by missing the meet. That was the last time I knowingly joined a team of any kind if I knew that I wasn't going to take it seriously and give it my best effort. Others simply deserve your best when they are depending on you and putting their trust in you.

Taking Action

- Do you make it a point to do your best when you take on a challenge? If so, what motivates you to do so? If not, why not?

- Do you notice and appreciate when others give their best for you?

- Has anyone ever let you down by putting in a poor effort on your behalf? How did it make you feel? Do you want to make others feel that way?

- Develop a list of ways that doing less than your best will produce a better outcome for anyone. You won't need much paper.

- Before agreeing to a new commitment, do you carefully consider your ability to contribute the necessary time and energy to give it your best and do it right?

- Have you ever overcommitted yourself and then regretted it because you weren't able to follow through at a level you felt good about?

Chapter 13
The Big Decisions in Life

You will have a number of big decisions to make in life. What college should you attend? What should you major in? What job should you take? Where should you live? Who should you marry? Most of the time these decisions will be difficult to make and you'll spend a lot of time stressed, and even scared, as you decide which way to go. You'll know your life will never be the same once you finalize a choice, so you'll be extra cautious. You'll try to be sure that you're making the right decision.

However, you'll never have the level of certainty you desire because there usually isn't any way to know for sure what the right decision is. There will always be some doubt and uncertainty. The key is that once you make a decision, commit to it. Once you're sure that the evidence is overwhelmingly leaning toward one option over the others, go with it. You usually can't remove all doubt or prove exhaustively that one option is truly correct. Life isn't that simple, and neither are the big decisions you'll make.

I once read a very interesting book about how people make choices. One of the central points of the book is that studies show that when people have more options, they not only have a harder time making a decision, they are also less happy with their decision. How can that be? With more choices, shouldn't you only have more ways to get to the best choice?

The point the book makes is that in addition to having more options, you have more ways to see where, overall, the best choice is weak. For example, you are in the market to buy a house. You've looked at a house that is horrible, but has a terrific mountain view. You know you never, ever would want that house, but whatever house you do pick, if it doesn't have that stunning view, now you know what you're missing. That will eat at you and make you wonder if there isn't a choice out there that has the house you want *and* the view. The more houses you see, the more characteristics you add to your ideal house and the harder it will be to find it.

So, what should you do? I wouldn't ever suggest you settle or take the easy route. This is especially true when it comes to decisions as important as where to live or who to marry. At the same time, there is a point where what you're looking at is such a solid choice that it starts to seem awfully risky to turn away from it in hopes of finding a better choice later. Sure, if you find a job you'd rate as one in a million, there is always a chance you might find one that's one in ten million. However, is the very slight improvement worth the risk of losing out completely? Is the extra stress and hassle and risk of pursuing the one in ten million jobs worth missing out on the one in a million opportunity? Probably not.

I am actually laughing at myself as I write this chapter because I feel quite hypocritical. I am NOT good at making a decision without driving myself crazy over it. I want to analyze, compare, and ensure I make the right decision. As I get older, I have realized how negative this trait can be in some situations. I have tried, with some success, to control it. If you share my ability to overthink decisions, please try to learn to control this obsession earlier than I did. I have spent so much time agonizing over what TV to buy, for example, that I know the extra bit of money I saved or the extra feature I got really wasn't worth my time. Worse yet, just like that book suggested, all the research always makes me painfully aware of any small option that I did not end up with as part of my final choice.

Divorce has become a regular occurrence in society today and this is a very unfortunate trend. I think a large part of the problem is that many people enter into marriage without being truly committed. They assume they can just get a divorce if it doesn't work out. That's a horrible way to enter into a marriage. If you don't believe that you're making a permanent decision, you shouldn't get married at all. Marriage isn't something to simply try out.

People are also getting married much later in life than they used to. I think this is partly because everyone wants to find the perfect person for them. They may have someone terrific, but they are worried that there is an even better match out there. They may also figure they're too young at the time they find someone who is a good match for them and that someone else just as good will come along when they're ready to commit later in life.

I believe that when you meet someone you're convinced you would marry if you were at a different point in life, you should do it right then. I don't care if you're only twenty-four-years-old, you're unemployed, or you're planning to move across the country. Don't let those things stop you from sticking with the right person. You can work through things if the fit is right. I've known people who have deep regret over someone they let go.

Let's go back to the discussion about choices. A long time ago, people lived in small towns. The person they married was chosen from a very limited pool of people. Divorce was very rare. Sure, there were probably some unhappy people, but for the most part, it seemed to work. I believe this is partly because people knew that they had limited options. They couldn't afford to let someone go who was a good match for them because they were certain that they wouldn't have a better match coming along. They knew what all their choices were, so they committed and never looked back.

In today's connected society, you can meet thousands of potential partners. No matter how good a fit someone is, you know that there are thousands more people you can meet if you take the time. Focusing on all the unknown choices that you haven't met, instead of the one in front of you, can cause you much more stress and pain over the long run. Making a decision that feels right will be awfully hard to beat.

A Few Examples from My Past

One example where an option bothered me relentlessly was when we bought a new house. We had put an offer in on a house a few miles away from where we landed, but it didn't work out. That house was on a lake with water views on two sides, a private backyard, a deck, and a dock. The outside of the house was amazing. However, the inside wasn't ideal. It was very nice, but much less open than the house we ended up with, and the basement was unfinished.

I know the house we bought was the right one for us because it has so many advantages over the other house—the biggest weakness is the lot. It has always bugged me that we couldn't have our house on the lake, even though that isn't an option. Sometimes when we drove past the other house, I'd point and say, "There's that house across the water." My family would be annoyed with me and I'd be annoyed with myself. It was silly to keep thinking about that house. All it did was cause me stress. I had fallen for the trap of seeing too many options and focusing on the one option missing in my choice, rather than all the good things that were present. Please be better than I was and just enjoy a good decision.

I've also burdened myself with needless stress over jobs. I've learned that once you start to consider leaving a company, you've crossed a line that is hard to retreat from. Somehow, admitting that you're not fully committed starts a pattern where you begin to notice all the bad things about your job and all the good things about other opportunities. I think there is something more at work, too. The more options you see, the less perfect your current job looks. My policy was that I wouldn't talk to a recruiter or colleague about a new job unless I was ready to leave. Why? Once you start looking, you'll see something you're missing that you could have by making a switch. However, you might not see all the downsides of the new job so quickly, and could end up regretting the decision.

I've heard of jobs that were a horrible fit for me, but each had some amazing feature. It might have had a super high pay package, it might be a "cool" company, it might have had some great benefits, or it might have been in a great location. Any job might be easy to dismiss as a bad choice overall. Yet, somehow, each one helped point out another "deficiency" in my current job. I'd eventually turn negative toward my current job. Nothing had changed except that I became aware of a range of jobs that I didn't really want, but that had a feature that I did want. It is crazy how it works to twist your mind.

I suggest you avoid allowing yourself to consider alternatives to any of your major decisions unless you truly want to change your decision. Otherwise you may open a can of worms that can cause you much stress and regret. Worse yet, you may prevent yourself from making a terrific decision. Once that happens, you may realize that your initial choice was far better than it seemed.

Taking Action

- How do you go about making the big decisions in your life?

- Have you ever fallen into the trap of looking for "just one more option" again and again before making a choice? How did the process end?

- Next time you have a big decision to make, consider making a list of the things that are most important to you and those that are least important. Do this before doing any research. Then, objectively assess your options against that list.

- Have you ever missed out completely on an opportunity because you couldn't make a decision? If you later regretted it, what could you do differently next time?

- Have you or anyone that you know ever changed a major decision due to another option becoming available and then later regretted it? Was it possible to return to the initial decision, or was it too late?

Chapter 14
Deciding What Challenges to Take On

In life, you will probably find more things that interest you and you'd like to do more than you can actually do. There is only so much time in a day and, in our technology-centric world, time has become, perhaps, the most valuable commodity people have. When I grew up, there were still times when people would take a break for a day, relax, and really do nothing. Today, there seems to be pressure, even from a young age, to be busy all the time. Just as you need sleep to let your body recover, you also need some downtime to let your mind recover.

Even in high school, you'll be faced with choices to make. Do you play sports? Join the band? Take art classes? Do volunteer work? And those are just a sample of the choices. The fact is that you can't possibly do all of the things you want to do, no matter how much you'd like to. You're going to have to choose a reasonable number of activities to pursue. If you want to be very good at what you do, you'll need to limit the number of things you choose to pursue even further. You can't become a champion at everything. It takes too much practice, time, and energy. You can try to be a champion of the few things you enjoy most, or you can dabble in many things and accept that you'll never reach the top levels. It is a choice between having more focus or more variety. There is no wrong answer, but you'll have to decide which of those paths you prefer to take. One you've chosen a path, it will impact the decisions you make from that point forward.

It isn't always easy to make the decision to stop an activity. There will usually be others disappointed to lose you from their program. On the flip side, there will always be those offering another activity that you could get involved in. They may be disappointed if you don't agree to participate. It can be hard to say no, but you'll have to learn to do it. Once you enter the workforce, you'll continue to be given work and responsibilities until you say "no more." If you willingly accept everything thrown at you, you'll just keep getting more and more. Eventually, you'll have no choice but to scale your workload back or you'll burn yourself out. I have never been good at saying no and numerous times over the years, I have come very close to burning out at work. I have gotten better at pushing back as I have aged, and now I am much more comfortable suggesting that someone else be found to do a task if I truly don't have the time to do it.

It gets even harder once you have children. Not only does every activity parents participate in for themselves have options for getting more involved, so do their children's activities. Whenever a child joins a team, a club, or some other group, the requests for time from his or her parents to help support the organization begin. That isn't a bad thing and it is totally fair for parents to be asked. However, it isn't possible to help with every organization your family is a part of. It is necessary for parents to decide which things they'll support with extra effort and which ones they will not.

Work is perhaps the hardest place to say no. After all, you can lose your job if you say no too often or do it in the wrong way. You can also end up making yourself miserable. I know people that got themselves into situations where they had to work literally around the clock for short time periods to deliver all they had committed to. Sometimes this is unavoidable and part of the job when unforeseen circumstances pop up, but many times people bring it on themselves by not pushing back at yet one more request. There were times that I was in that same situation myself.

Small requests are the worst because it seems odd to say you can't find an hour or two over a few weeks. I have often agreed to write an article or review a presentation for someone because I figured I could find the time somewhere. The problem is that I often agreed to too many "just an hour or two" items and ended up working until midnight multiple nights taking care of all those little things. I would have been more productive in my job and in a better state mentally if I had turned down more of the small requests. The trick is to help the person making the request to understand why you are turning it down. To them, the request being made is small and shouldn't be a problem. Only you have the perspective of knowing about all the other small requests you've already agreed to.

The flip side of this theme is to appreciate what people do for you. It is amazing how much work can go into something as simple as organizing a neighborhood pool party. My wife volunteered to arrange social events for our neighborhood when my children were small. It took a lot of effort to arrange and prepare for the various events. Until you have the chance to organize a few things, you won't appreciate how much work and time it takes for what seems like a simple task. Something as simple as having a few people over for dinner takes planning, cooking, and cleaning. Organizing a neighborhood party requires sending out invitations, organizing food and activities, recruiting helpers, cleaning up, paying the bills, and more. It is important to appreciate and thank those who take on such tasks for your benefit.

This topic is worth reinforcing—the pressures to do more and more seem to grow continually. Think about the boundaries you'll set and focus on the activities and commitments that are most important to you. It is impossible to do everything and make everyone happy.

A Few Examples from My Past

When my son joined the Cub Scouts, there were many activities to participate in. My wife and I agreed to help plan some of the den outings and help with a few other activities as well. This was fine and made perfect sense. After all, the whole point of scouting is for parent and child to do things together and teach the boys what being part of a team and taking on more responsibilities is all about.

At the beginning of the second year, I was asked to head up the popcorn fundraiser. It occurred in the fall, which was one of my busier travel seasons, and involved a lot of time. I knew that if I agreed, I wouldn't have time to do it right and it would cause me a great deal of stress. Many details that I wouldn't have had time to think about during the workweek, would all impact the limited free time I had on the weekends. Although I felt bad doing it, I said no to the job. I just knew that I couldn't succeed, so it was the right thing to do. A few years earlier, I probably would have given in and accepted the role, and then regretted it. I wouldn't have had the time to do it the way I thought it should be done and I would have felt that I let down the scout troop and my family. It would have been a negative, stressful experience for me rather than a positive one.

Until I had a house and kids of my own, I honestly had no idea how much work my mother would do over the holidays. I would have all sorts of good food and fun when I went home to my parents' house for the holidays. I didn't understand at the time how hard my mom had to work to make those things happen for me. I know she often felt she took on too much. In retrospect, I wish I had been aware so that I could have suggested some actions that she no longer needed to do. There are also countless ways I could have done more to help her out.

Be sure to recognize those who go the extra mile to make something you participate in go smoothly. They'll appreciate it. When you're the one who does the work, you will, too, because you took on the challenge to get it done.

Taking Action

- Do you ever feel that you have overcommitted and have more to do than you can effectively handle? What led you to that point?

- Are you good at saying no to requests when you don't have time? What can you do to get better at it?

- Do you make a point to recognize the efforts that others make on your behalf? Should you recognize people more often?

- Have you ever seen someone you know stressed and frustrated over a commitment that should have been a fun and happy one because they didn't have the time and were overcommitted?

- Make a point of keeping track of all the little things you've committed to so that you can effectively assess if you can handle another addition when asked.

Part Three

Setting Priorities

Chapter 15
Put Your Family First

You are going to be faced with many choices in life. You will have to prioritize various needs, desires, and plans when one thing has to take precedence over another. It is common for this to cause issues with family. There are many things that can distract you from your family— work, sports, friends, or hobbies. In my experience, work is typically the one that causes the most problems. It is necessary to recognize when other things are getting in the way of family, no matter what they are.

The world in which your generation is starting their careers is a very different place than when my generation started, which was a very different place when my parents' generation started. In the days when my parents were starting out, it was generally accepted that one spouse (usually the wife) would stay home and take care of the kids while the other spouse (usually the husband) would work to pay for housing, food, and everything else. Most jobs had reasonable hours and it was expected and understood that people needed to have time with their families.

Part of the difference was certainly due to the fact that modern technologies didn't exist. There was really no way to do anything for work once you were home, so it made it easy to keep work and home separate. Once you were at home, you couldn't do anything about work without going all the way back to the office. It had to be an important need to go down that path. It was still largely that way when I started out. There was no Internet, no cell phones, and no laptops. In a pinch, such as after a big snowstorm, I could make a few phone calls from home, but that was about it. I actually found it relatively easy to balance things.

That had totally changed by the time I had children. I worked from home for many years when I wasn't traveling. I'd take a trip almost every week for a few days, but otherwise, I would be home. With all the technologies available, it was very difficult to leave work completely and just be home with my family. I had my laptop downstairs, my cell phone at my side, and people in many different time zones who had become accustomed to communicating about work at all hours of the day and night.

As you start in your own career and marriage, you'll need to give some serious consideration as to what is most important to you. One big decision will be whether or not you or your spouse will quit work and raise your kids. My wife and I decided to have her quit her job because we thought it would be best for our kids. We don't regret it. While it is true that we would have had more money with a second salary, we didn't think the money was worth having someone else effectively raising our kids for us.

Many people don't make the same decision we made. In some cases, people can't afford to have one person not working. I think more people in that situation should consider moving to a lower cost area where they could afford to have one spouse not working. It is also a fact that many people want to keep both spouses working for extra money and career purposes, not for survival purposes. In my opinion, that isn't the best choice. If you can afford to have a parent stay home, do it. It will be best for the children. That's my stance. In addition, if a spouse is going to stay home, be sure to plan for it. Don't take on debts that require both incomes, for example. Otherwise, you risk being forced to go down paths you did not want to go down.

I've seen many kids with very successful parents grow up to be a mess. I think much of it is because the parents were more concerned with being successful in their work and personal lives than with being successful at parenting. Part of what enabled me to have the success I have had is my parents being present when I was young to teach me things and demonstrate how to succeed. I believe that you, your spouse, and your children will be better off if you plan to have someone stay home full-time when your kids are young. I also hope that you will be prepared for life because of the sacrifices your parents made for you. My wife and I have never regretted the decision we made to have her stay home.

A second big area to focus on is how far the working spouse will go in pursuit of more money and success at work. I know many people who are very successful by business and career standards, but who are never around for their spouse and kids. To me, that's a shame. My wife and I regularly monitored if I was getting sucked into work too much because, unfortunately, it was a problem. When we felt I was, I would make some changes to adjust. I passed up various opportunities that would have been good career moves, but would have impacted the family too much. I wasn't willing to work 90-100 hours every week no matter what the pay. When I was single, I moved all over the country to take the best job I could get and to move ahead. Once I had children, I regularly turned down lucrative opportunities that would have required us to relocate or would have required me to be home even less than I already was. I didn't want to put my family through the stress of it.

Make your own choices on how to prioritize your family, but I strongly recommend that when you are in doubt, choose the option that will be the most family-friendly. You can voluntarily change jobs any time, or get fired or laid off, but your family is for keeps.

A Few Examples from My Past

When I was a baby, my dad was in the Navy and worked on nuclear submarines. This meant that he was at sea for three to six months at a time, with no trips back home and limited communication of any kind. At best, he received infrequent letters when the sub was docked somewhere that could send and receive mail. My dad didn't get to see me until I was six weeks old because he was at sea when I was born. Then, when I was about five months old, he had to go to sea for a few months again. That's when he decided to leave the Navy. He didn't want to be away like that anymore. He gave up his career in the Navy so that he could be home with our family. I do not recall him ever mentioning that he regretted the decision.

I grew up playing soccer. When my son was born, my ability to play was limited due to bad knees, but I was getting heavily into being a referee. When my son was a baby, I managed to referee a little bit, but did so far less than I had before he was born. Once my daughter was born, I realized that I just didn't have the time or energy to keep it up. I wasn't willing to miss a good chunk of a weekend day for my referee work when it meant missing quality time with my kids. With two of them vying for my time, it stretched me that much thinner. I stopped refereeing completely and never regretted it. Did I miss playing and refereeing? Sure, but I knew that I was doing something more important with my time, so it didn't bother me.

One last story deals with a colleague I once had who was an owner of a small company. He seemed to put work above family on a regular basis, even though he had several small children at home. During a conversation one evening, someone asked if he minded how much he had been away from home the prior few months. He replied that work came first. He and his wife both had agreed to it—he was going to do what it took to build the company, and later focus on family. I was shocked at how blunt and open he was about his priorities. I totally disagreed with his approach, but it was his right to choose it. If his wife was in agreement as well, that was their choice to make.

However, I've always wondered how his kids felt about that decision. They weren't really given a choice. Who knows if his lack of priority on them caused them issues. They probably picked up on the fact that they were second to his job. While he did end up making quite a good payout for his efforts, I am not convinced it was worth it. I would have given up such a payday to get the time with my kids when they were small. Don't let your career blind you to the needs of your family. If you aren't willing to sacrifice for your family, then don't have one in the first place.

Taking Action

- Do you feel your parents put you first? If you do, seek to emulate them. If not, consider whether you believe you'd be better off if they had. If so, use that as motivation to be different with your kids.

- Do you know anyone whose parents clearly don't put them first? How does that make them feel? Even as an outsider, how do you feel about the situation?

- Have you determined what priorities you would like to have once you have a family? Discuss those priorities with a potential spouse before you get married. You need to be in sync from the start.

- Would you like one parent to stay home when you have children? Begin planning now. Start saving, consider moving somewhere with a low cost of living, and keep your expenses down to ease the transition from two paychecks to one.

Chapter 16
Do What is Right, Not What is Easy

Often in life, you'll be faced with a choice when you can take the easy way out or you can spend some extra time, money, and/or effort to do what's right. It can be very tempting to take the easy way out. This is especially true if you think nobody is watching and nobody will notice. However, YOU will know if you've taken a shortcut and over time, the more often you take shortcuts, the easier it will be to take one again. Eventually, you may lose your ability to distinguish between what's right and what's easy and your life and your character will suffer. There are many situations where what's right and what's easy differ. I'll discuss three here, even though there are certainly more.

The first situation arises when effort of some kind is required. For example, perhaps you need to repair a fence. There is the right way to do it (so it lasts a long time), and many easy ways to do it (so the fence is no longer lying on the ground), but it really isn't fixed. If you're repairing the fence for yourself, and you want to take an easy way out, that can be ok as long as it only impacts you. However, if you are repairing the fence for someone else, they will expect you to do it right. When you agree to repair the neighbor's fence that you broke, for example, you owe it to them to do it correctly. Do what you would expect them to do if they had broken your fence. A shoddy job is not acceptable; hold yourself to a higher standard.

The second situation involves finances. When you have agreed to provide certain items to someone, for whatever purpose, you owe them good quality items that you believe will meet their needs. It isn't right to buy something cheap just to save money and yet be able to claim you met your obligation. For example, if you offer to provide a vacuum cleaner to a nursing home as a charitable gift, you owe it to them to provide a good, high quality vacuum and not a junky one that won't hold up in an environment of heavy use. Similarly, if you agree to buy food for a party, don't show up with a bucket of fast food chicken nuggets. Purchase or prepare something nice that others will enjoy.

The third situation, where feelings or emotions are involved, is often the hardest. There will be times when it would be easy to avoid an uncomfortable situation by either ignoring certain facts or avoiding certain discussions. These are the kinds of situations where you will really be put to the test. An extreme situation would be when you see a friend steal something. The easy thing to do is ignore it and justify it by thinking that the friend has never done it before and will never do it again. The right thing to do is to confront them and possibly turn them in.

Another situation is one where you know someone is interested in you romantically and you don't feel the same way. The easy thing is to hope they'll figure it out eventually and move on. The right thing to do is to sit them down and let them know where they stand.

These types of situations will be the true test of your character. Having a difficult discussion, delivering bad news, or providing feedback that isn't what someone wanted to hear is not fun. No normal person enjoys doing such things, but these situations are inevitable in life. Part of being a responsible adult is to accept that you'll need to do what's right in circumstances when you want to do anything but what is right. As with some of the other traits discussed in this book, having a reputation as a person who will do what's right—in terms of labor, money, and relationships—will help you immensely in life. Best of all, you'll be proud that you are living up to a high standard.

A Few Examples from My Past

When it comes to effort, we put a lot of trust in people such as building contractors and mechanics. A good friend of mine had a father who was a housing contractor. My friend confirms that the common belief that many contractors do shoddy work is true. He believed his dad was successful because he did what was right and didn't take shortcuts. It is easy to use cheap wire or skip some steps when walls will cover up the shortcut taken so that nobody would ever know. His dad never did that. People appreciated the quality of his work and knew they could count on him to do the work correctly. As a result, he was quite successful. The best part is that because his dad operated that way, my friend learned to do the same. His father provided a solid example and my friend followed it.

When it comes to finances, it also makes sense to do the right thing. Over the years, I've tried to go the cheap route on a number of purchases. I usually regretted it. Once I bought a weed eater because it was cheap and I didn't have many weeds or edging to do. Once I got it home, I realized that it was so flimsy that it didn't work at all for what I needed. I did what was easy to save a few dollars, wasted my money on something that didn't provide me any value and, in the end, had to buy a better version. I should have done what was right and purchased a quality product in the first place. You may have to plan and save to buy the quality you need, especially if a big purchase is involved, but it is better to go without until you can do it right.

You can often tell when someone did things on the cheap. You may enter someone's home and see either very cheap fixtures or very sloppy workmanship. It reflects poorly on the house. Unless you are truly financially strapped, it is important to maintain a house with quality repairs and updates. If not, the value of the house will drop and you'll pay the price one day when you want to sell it, as well as when the substandard items and workmanship need repair sooner than they would have otherwise.

When feelings and emotions are involved, difficult situations can easily arise. Often, you have to put yourself through some discomfort to do what's right. A few years before I started dating my wife, I was dating someone else. I was really into her and even thought about marrying her. I still remember the night she dropped the bomb on me that she didn't see a long-term future with me anymore. She thought we should just end things immediately. I tried to talk her into reconsidering, but she stuck to her guns and broke up with me. At the time, I was quite hurt and didn't understand how it had happened, but eventually I realized that we weren't right for each other. I respect and appreciate that she chose to end it quickly and openly once she realized that first. She did what was right. Had she given in to my suggestion to reconsider, we would have drawn out the inevitable and made it even more difficult.

I have known many people who stay in a relationship when they know it isn't going anywhere. Sometimes both parties will acknowledge it isn't going anywhere, but neither of them is willing to do the difficult and right thing of ending it. They just ignore the obvious as if the problem will magically go away. Months or years of their lives are wasted just so they don't have to explicitly end the relationship and deal with the pain and discomfort these conversations and actions will bring.

Similarly uncomfortable situations can arise if you have a friend who is using drugs or otherwise making bad choices in life. You owe it to that person to confront them and try to convince them to change their direction. It won't always work, but a friend will try. If everyone sits by and says nothing, it is much more likely that the person will continue on their errant path. By having friends intervene and try to help, the friend may just pull themselves back together.

Taking Action

- Identify a time in your past when you took the easy way out. Why did you do it? How did it turn out?

- Can you think of an example in your past when you did the right thing even though it was difficult? How did you feel? How did the people you impacted feel?

- When something is being done for you, do you want others to do it right or take an easy way out? Why would you do for others differently than what you expect for yourself?

- Especially with something important, take a moment to consider explicitly what the right way to proceed is and what the easy ways out are. Be sure to force yourself down the right path.

- Do you know anyone who always seems to do the right thing? How does that make you feel about them?

Chapter 17
Plan for the Worst

It would be terrific if everything in life always went smoothly and we never faced adversity. However, that isn't how the world works. I believe it is important to be optimistic and keep a positive viewpoint about any given situation. At the same time, I think it is important to consider the negative possibilities as well. If you consider negative possibilities up front, you will be much better prepared to handle them should they arise.

I believe that one of the most common reasons people end up with a big failure is that they didn't plan for the worst. Perhaps they very effectively planned for the best, maybe even for the good, but they didn't plan for the bad or the worst. When things turn negative, they are blindsided and unprepared. When you get yourself into that type of situation, failure becomes a very real option.

In anything important, build contingencies into your plans for the unexpected. To the extent you can identify specific things that might go wrong, account for them. Also include some extra padding for totally unexpected trouble. For example, if you are embarking upon a remodel of your kitchen, many, many things can go wrong. Suppliers might be late delivering, which causes delays. Hidden problems with pipes or wiring might be uncovered during demolition. One of the workers might make a big mistake.

The point is that a major remodel almost never happens without a glitch. If you've planned your remodel in a way that your timeline is the fastest possible timeline and you have no money set aside for anything unexpected, you can quickly get into a bad situation. It is best to build in extra time and set aside some extra cash to deal with the unexpected. In those cases where all goes according to plan, you will be ahead of schedule and budget, which is great! If there are problems, you'll still be fine.

Many people fail to consider the risks when they make decisions in life. Even deciding where to live requires some serious thought. If you rent or purchase a place to live that requires a huge portion of your income, you may not have enough left over to pay for other unexpected expenses that arise. What if your car needs major repairs? What if you get very sick and can't work for a while? You can't live your life in fear of such things, but you can live your life in a way in which you plan and prepare for such things. By keeping your living expenses down and building up an emergency cash reserve, you'll be able to handle unexpected bumps in the road. You'll also have comfort in knowing that you have that cushion.

In today's world, most people live very well relative to historical norms. We also face some risks that most people don't think about. Vast majorities of people don't have the ability to produce their own food and are totally dependent on the grocery store. This works well when everything is operating normally. However, it can lead to fast trouble when disaster strikes. While we need supplies from stores, those stores carry only a limited amount of supplies at any one time. A continual flow of merchandise is necessary to keep the store running. If the deliveries are cut off, a grocery store can be out of food within a few days. This is especially true if there is a panic for supplies due to a disaster or emergency of some kind.

The average family today doesn't plan for the worst when it comes to household supplies. If a disaster strikes, the family will be in trouble very quickly. This has led many people to purchase emergency supplies so that they can survive an emergency, such as severe weather or a fuel shortage. Similar to having an emergency stash of cash, an emergency stash of food, water, batteries, blankets, first aid items, and other basic supplies are stored. This is very smart because emergency cash will not do any good if nothing is available to purchase. Just like life insurance or fire insurance, we all hope that we will never need to rely on emergency supplies, but it is smart to be prepared. In your life, you will be much better off if you plan for the worst from the beginning, even while you enjoy results that are usually far from the worst.

A Few Examples from My Past

One reason I think I have been successful in my career is because I have always planned for the worst. In my work providing consulting services, each project has its own risks. Just like a kitchen remodel, there are always things that can go wrong. I know many people in my line of work who have had major project failures. People who have led major failed efforts are often very smart and good at what they do. However, they get into trouble when they don't consider the potential trouble spots up front. When a project hits trouble, they aren't prepared and the project starts sliding downhill fast.

I have often been accused of overthinking things. I can't argue that—it's true. However, at times my method of overthinking has been a great benefit, even if it can be also annoying. I always make it a point to think about all of the potential trouble spots in a project. To account for those potential problems, I adjust the schedules and budgets I am proposing. I don't adjust the project plan to reflect that every potential problem will actually happen—that would drive the cost much too high. Rather, once

I have a list of potential problems and my estimated probability that they might occur, I build in consideration for the trouble that seems reasonable to expect given those facts.

I also determine what course of action can be taken if the problem occurs. This enables me to respond quickly and help the project team to work around the issues that arise. Much of the advance thought I give may seem like wasted energy because most of the problems don't occur, but for those that do occur, my effort is well rewarded. Of course, there are also times that a problem occurs that I had not anticipated. When that happens, my method of building in time and money for some unexpected risks provides a cushion to deal with these situations, too.

Planning-for the worst has also paid off for me in my travels. When bad weather is projected during a trip, I don't simply hope the weather stays clear. Instead, I take a few minutes before I leave to look into alternative flights and consider how I can rearrange my calendar and priorities if the bad weather actually hits. This way, if the weather causes trouble, I already have some plans of action. While many people on my flight are caught off guard with a major delay or cancellation, I am ready to spring into action immediately and start working my contingency plans.

I have often booked alternative flights before others have realized the need to do so. In such situations, it is like a game of musical chairs. Those who are late in trying to obtain alternate accommodations often find their options are already gone. For example, if there are only 30 seats available on the remaining flights today, but 100 people were scheduled for the flight that was just cancelled, only the first 30 people who try to grab the remaining seats will get one. By knowing what to ask for ahead of time, I can pick up the phone and call immediately. Even the five or ten minutes it takes others to figure out their options causes them to fight for the seats remaining after I lock in mine.

Taking Action

- Have you ever gotten into a real bind because you didn't plan for potential problems? What was the result?

- Do you develop contingency plans and think through potential hurdles when you start a major undertaking? If not, why not?

- Have you or a friend escaped a situation that had the potential to be very bad, due to being prepared to respond quickly and effectively?

- What can you do better to plan for the worst in the future?

- Planning for the worst is not being pessimistic or a waste of time. Think of it like insurance. Even when your effort isn't needed, you still have peace of mind knowing that you are protected if problems arise.

Chapter 18
Keep Some Variety in Your Life

This topic overlaps a little with putting family first, but not entirely. In this chapter, I'm going to take things in a slightly different direction. I've already talked about keeping family first, so now let's look at the other aspects of your life where it is also important to keep some balance.

There is an old phrase, "All work and no play makes Jack a dull boy." I also suggest that "all play and no work" won't lead to a very positive personality or lifestyle either. The fact is that you're going to need to work, and you're going to need to do some things outside of work. The ratio of work to play may vary, but you'll do well to keep balance in all areas of your life.

It is easy to envision that working 100 hours a week and doing nothing else is going to wear you down. To keep a balance, it is a good idea to have a range of hobbies, sports, activities, and friends. If you only focus on one or two things, and if for some reason you can no longer do those things, you'll be in a bit of a bind. What will you do to fill the void? It's not that you won't be able to find other things to enjoy if it becomes necessary, but if you've been cultivating other interests over time, it will make the transition easier.

I think that balance is needed in many areas. Try a couple of musical instruments before putting a lot of time into just one or two. Try a range of sports before focusing on a couple that you really enjoy. Go to a variety of places for vacations. Try a variety of restaurants before starting to return to your favorites. Even if you have a favorite restaurant or vacation spot, add a little variety to your life. Do not just go to one place all the time, but occasionally test out a new place instead of sticking to your favorites. It might just end up being your new favorite. You'll never find your next and newest favorite without trying someplace new.

Balance is important because it helps you to become proficient at a much wider range of skills. The more skills you have in life, the more opportunities you'll be able to take advantage of. When my kids were young, they were very open to trying different things and liked to participate in a variety of activities. I hope that they'll continue to do that as they get older, and even as they have their own families.

You probably know people who always want to do the same thing with the same people day after day and week after week. I'm not saying that those people can't be happy and don't enjoy life; I just think that they might be even happier and enjoy life even more if they broadened their horizons a little bit. Keeping a balance and adding some variety in your life means you'll have a chance to learn more new things and to find something new that you enjoy as much as other things you already do.

A Few Examples from My Past

I probably focused too much on soccer when I was in my twenties and thirties. I loved playing soccer and put most of my activity time outside of work towards it. I really didn't think about the fact that I wouldn't be able to play forever. As my knees gave way and my kids were born, I quickly went from playing almost every week year-round to not playing at all. I didn't know what to do to replace the spot that soccer had in my life. That's when it first hit me—perhaps I had focused too much on one thing. By then it was too late to do anything about it. If I had developed some additional hobbies more fully over time, my transition would have been far easier.

I started running more than I had in the years prior, but that too bothered my knees and legs. There were a few years when I was usually injured or operating at half speed. I got totally out of shape and felt bad. Eventually, I decided I had to shake things up and get into some new types of physical activities. I started bike riding, hiking, running on trails instead of pavement, and working with a variety of challenging exercise videos. I was amazed by how much I enjoyed the new activities. If I had maintained more balance during the previous years, I could have made a smooth transition from my soccer career, rather than having those years of difficulty.

I've known people who were totally focused on just one thing. If someone actually has the talent and desire to pursue that activity for a living, that's one thing, but if not, it can be very limiting. What happens if you only focus on a single sport and then you get a major injury that knocks you out? What if your focus is on an art form that requires exacting movements, and then your hands get injured? Not only will keeping a balance be beneficial in the short run, it can be a huge help in adapting to life changes in the long run. Plus, having different activities that you enjoy adds more variety to your life, which is always a positive thing. Feeling like you are stuck in a rut isn't a fun place to be.

Here's another example of maintaining balance. When I travelled, frequently I would go out to dinner with groups of co-workers who were also in town. The people varied based on where I was, but there was usually a group outing of some sort for dinner. I always enjoyed finding local restaurants to try. I'd purposely seek out the well-known dive with great food when it was left up to me, but many people didn't want to do that. Surprisingly, many people wanted to go to the same old chain restaurants night after night. The food wasn't bad, but it was the same food I could have had back home a mile from my house. Why not try something different when the opportunity arises? Think of all the great meals my co-workers missed out on. Their fear of the infrequent bad meal at an unknown restaurant made them miss all the good ones.

Another advantage of diversifying your activities is that you'll have more opportunities to find a common interest with loved ones. Chances are that your spouse won't share all of your interests, nor will your children. For example, my wife had no interest in soccer whatsoever. That meant that my time spent with soccer was something I did without her. If you have multiple activities and hobbies, chances are better that you'll find at least one you can share with any given person. I have found it to be quite enjoyable once common interests are found. For example, my wife, my children, and I all enjoy taking hikes and riding bikes together. It is a nice way to have some good family time and get out of the house at the same time.

Too much of anything can be bad. Seek out some variety. Aim to have balance in all aspects of your life. The more dimensions in which you have balance, the less impact adverse events will cause in your life. You'll naturally be able to adjust better and you'll be happier, too.

Taking Action

- Do you think that you keep a good balance in your life? If not, what are some changes that you can make to create a better balance?

- Do you get stuck in ruts because you always stick to the same routines, or do you continuously seek out new experiences? Adding some variety to your routines now and then can be very beneficial.

- If you suddenly couldn't participate in your favorite activity anymore, would that cause a serious issue, or can you easily see how you'd fill the time? Work toward getting yourself to the latter position.

- Assess the level of balance you have in your life at least once per year. Then, make adjustments as necessary.

Chapter 19
Helping the Less Fortunate

When our kids were young we instituted the policy of having them divide their money into three categories or "buckets." There is a "Spend" bucket, which can be spent on anything desired. There is a "Save" bucket, which goes to savings for college or other future needs. There is a "Give" bucket, which is for donating to charity. This concept can be credited to Dave Ramsey, who is currently a popular expert on personal finance. The last bucket is the focus of this chapter.

How big should your Give bucket be and how should you allocate the money? That isn't an easy question to answer and each person will need to determine what he or she is comfortable with. The key is to have a Give bucket for your entire life. Donating to charity is something that people have always done. I consider it a way to show thankfulness for what you have, as well as a way to help others in times of need. Giving is taken so seriously that many churches request a "tithe," which means that 10 percent of everything you make goes to the church. Even people who tithe to a church often donate additional money outside of the church because they feel it is a moral imperative to do so.

Hopefully, you'll never be in a position to require charitable support. However, if you do end up in that situation, you can feel better about receiving charity if you've supported others over time. In that sense, charity can be considered a type of insurance. You give when you can to help others. You take some back if you need it. If you never need it, consider yourself lucky. You can feel good that you did the right thing by helping others when you were able to. It is wonderful if you are fortunate enough to live your entire life without ever needing charitable support.

In addition to giving money, the gift or your time and services can have a huge impact. If you don't have money to give, become a volunteer. Taking action and getting personally involved in a charitable activity will lead to a much better perspective than simply donating money. When you don't have a lot of money to give, giving your time might be the only option you have. Even when you do have money, consider giving your time, too.

There are so many types of charities and so many important missions you can support that it is overwhelming. It isn't possible to help everyone who asks. You're going to need to pick a few areas that are important to you and support those areas. Our family chose to support children's charities and our church as our main giving buckets. We would still support other charities from time to time, but we made sure we allocated the base amount for church and children's programs first.

I'd rather give substantial gifts to a few charities than to give small gifts to many. That is just my preference and it is not the only way to do it. I like writing a few big checks while knowing some of the specific needs the funds will address. Also, charities have overhead expenses. A large percentage of the funds from small gifts end up being allocated to processing expenses since they are the same per donation, no matter what the dollar amount. As a result, the larger your individual gift, the more effective it will be.

I also believe that private charity is far more efficient and impactful than government assistance. We all pay taxes to fund government assistance programs. Unfortunately, many of them aren't well run and, in my opinion, frequently the money isn't efficiently spent. If some of that tax money was left in the hands of people to provide to private charity, I believe we'd be much better off. There are those who disagree with me on this, but it is how I feel.

The reason I bring it up is that as tax burdens rise, there is less in your pocket. That means less to donate to private charities. No matter how high your taxes go, continue to find ways to support private charity. I don't like to think about a society where the only charity available is the government. With each tax increase, the government takes over a larger share of charity, and private charities keep a smaller share since people have less to give. Unchecked, a time will come that private charities are unable to survive and the only option remaining in a time of need will be the government. Throughout history, societies that have reached that status have not fared well. I hope that you'll do your part to keep private charity alive and well.

A Few Examples from My Past

When I was in my twenties, I didn't think much about charity. It wasn't that I had dismissed the idea of giving to charity; it was simply that I didn't think about it and therefore didn't donate very much. When someone asked for a donation, I would write a modest check, but I didn't really have a plan. This meant that if no one asked me to donate for a while, I wouldn't give for a while either. I was aware that my parents gave money regularly and they encouraged me to do it, too. However, I just didn't focus on it for a number of years. I regret that now. It wasn't until I got married that my focus on charity started to increase and I got to a point where I felt I was giving as much as I should. I hope that by reading this, you'll not lose focus as I did. Have a giving plan every year.

One area I have struggled with over the years is how much to give each year. So many different guidelines are offered. Even in the case of a tithe to a church, I was never clear if a tithe was supposed to be 10 percent of income before tax or 10 perecent of income after tax. Most people who are serious about giving to charity would probably agree that a good target budget is at least 5-10 percent of your income after taxes. The key is to budget and plan for it just as you do with other expenses. That way, you'll always have the money to give.

At the end of every year, I ask myself if the amount I gave during the year makes me a little uncomfortable because the amount was so large. If so, I have probably given enough. If you only give what amounts to your pocket change, you aren't being as charitable as you can be. Give enough so that you notice it in your budget, and you are forced to forego some things for yourself in order to meet your charitable giving budget. Being slightly uncomfortable validates that I really gave enough to feel it.

One thing our family never worried about was getting formal recognition for our giving. The reward of giving should be enough by itself. To me, if you give just to get your name on a wall plaque or to be recognized in public at a dinner, that taints your gift. You are getting something other than satisfaction out of the gift, so it isn't totally charitable. If you give purely to be charitable and just happen to end up with another benefit, then that is different. I am only uncomfortable when part of the reason for the gift is to receive the benefit. I have also always been uncomfortable with published lists of donors that include their level of giving. I have only allowed my name to be on them because, realistically, few people pay attention and actually notice my name on the list.

Make sure you give for giving's sake and not to get anything except satisfaction for yourself. I believe that what you give should be a private matter. Don't tell your friends or neighbors how much you give to make yourself look good. Keep it to yourself. You'll know you've done the right thing and that should be enough.

Taking Action

- Have you thought recently about why you should give time and money to charity and why it is important to you?

- Do you have a line item for charity in your budget, whether formally or informally? If not, add one today.

- Have you identified the types of charities that you feel most strongly about supporting? It is easier to stay motivated to give when you've found some causes you really want to support.

- Do you give enough that the amount makes you a little uncomfortable? If not, try to give more. You should feel an impact.

- What can you do to give more of your time and/or money in the coming year?

Chapter 20
Speak Up and Take Charge

Over time, you'll end up in many situations where it isn't clear what a group is supposed to be doing. People may sit and look around at each other waiting for direction. Or, someone will ask for opinions and nobody will offer one. If you are always one of the ones sitting silently, frequently things won't work out in ways that satisfy you. Honestly, you can't really complain if you didn't do anything to guide the outcome.

At the same time, don't be a person who is always in everyone's face and being overly aggressive and pushy. People will stop listening to what you have to say and will go out of their way to prevent you from getting your way. You'll have made it personal, which is highly counterproductive.

Identify when an issue is something you really care about and when it is not. When you really don't care, sit back, and let someone who does care step in and take the lead. Even if you do care, decide if the situation is one that is really worth taking a stand on and going to battle for, or not. You might prefer to go to an ice cream shop rather than a yogurt shop. If some in the group are pressing for yogurt, is it that big of a deal to go along? Limiting the use of your influence to drive outcomes when it counts most helps ensure you'll have the greatest impact when you most need it. People will listen more to your arguments when they know you reserve them for things you feel most strongly about.

Many people are never comfortable stepping into a leadership role or taking a public stand. That's okay if that's truly who they are, but they won't achieve much influence. Often times, they will hitch a ride with whoever makes a stand first. Why shouldn't that stand be from you? If you are confident in your position, you can often get things to go your way simply by expressing your view. It won't always work, but it will work far more often than you'd expect. This will be especially true if you state your case with confidence, facts, and logic on your side.

There are many situations in life where I can honestly see both sides of an issue. I may feel strongly one way, but I am able to acknowledge that someone else might disagree, given their different view of the world. Again, when people are looking for direction, they'll often fall in behind whoever is first to make a strong case. When you can see that the other side has arguments that will resonate with people, it is essential to make your case first. If not, you are risking that someone else will use the arguments that you see for the other side to make that case instead. Once people have decided that one side seems very solid, it will take a substantial amount of persuasion to get them to switch that view. By planting your view first, you greatly increase the chances your view will win.

This trend is most obvious in very difficult or uncomfortable situations. Most people don't like conflict. I don't either. Sometimes you need to have conflict, however. When an issue is raised and people are uncomfortable, most will sit quietly hoping someone else will speak first. When someone finally does speak up, many will be relieved that someone else presented their view for them. If you are recognized as someone who speaks honestly and factually, then you have the ability to sway decisions your direction. People will respect your courage and conviction.

Sometimes things will not go your way. You may even regret having spoken if nobody backs you up. Sometimes, that's the price you must pay for taking a stand. Over time, the pain of the occasions it went badly will be dwarfed by the gains you achieved when it went well. At least you can say you tried in those times you lost. I'd rather try to win and end up losing than sit quietly and lose without ever trying to win. I hope you'll adopt that viewpoint as your own.

A Few Examples from My Past

When I was in high school, the county decided to turn my school into a hi-tech magnet school and end its role as a regular school. Once the decision to migrate the school to a magnet was made, it had to be determined exactly how to execute the transition. Should my school close right away and send my class to our rival school for senior year? Should we let the current freshmen finish out and be alone their last year? Or did something in between work best?

I was one of a handful of student representatives on the committee that would decide over a period of a few months how to phase out my high school. The principals of both schools, some teachers, and a variety of parents were also on the committee. The committee met for several months on a regular basis to hash things out. We students tended to have stronger feelings than most of the adults, which would be expected, but it was intimidating to sit with all of them in a room. They ran the meetings in a very serious and formal fashion, which I was not accustomed to. Knowing that what I said could get me in hot water with people I didn't want to be in hot water with was also a concern.

When we finally narrowed it down to a couple of options, the student representatives had a very strong preference about how our school should close. The students from our rival school had strong opinions as well, which weren't totally in sync with ours. The parents and administrators were all over the map. I remember getting ready to go to the meeting where we would debate which of the identified options would be put in place. The students from my school decided we had to make our case. If we didn't speak up then, we'd miss the chance. As the meeting started, we made our plea and explained our reasons. In the end, the committee decided to go with our view. We had made a credible case, we would be the most impacted, and as a result, others acknowledged that we should have some input. Had we not spoken up, who knows what would have happened. Our school transitioned in a way that we believed worked best. I credit that, in part, to the fact that we made our case strongly and first during that critical meeting.

Another example took place in my church. I was on the finance committee of the church just as a massive financial crisis hit the entire country full force. Our donations were down, we had many bills to pay, and we knew we were not going to bring in what we needed to meet our obligations that year. Many, if not most churches were in the same situation. After a few years of purposely borrowing money via a line of credit to invest in improvements and growth in the church and its programs, for the first time we borrowed money just to stay afloat. With lines of credit drying up quickly, we knew we couldn't keep heading down this path.

The alternatives were unappealing. We cut program budgets to the bone; facility expenses really couldn't be lowered. After all, you have to light and heat the church. That left us with staff salaries. We had a range of staff, but it became apparent to me that we couldn't keep them all, and probably couldn't keep any of them at their current salaries. This was a very unpleasant reality.

As we went through the budget cycle, there were those who didn't want to face the reality. They wanted us to "have faith," "believe in our mission," and keep spending just as we had been. A few of us thought we'd be bankrupt in a year or two if we did that. We eventually had to speak up and suggest cutting the staff budget. This would lead to the complete loss of some staff positions, as well as reducing the salaries of some who would remain.

This was a very emotional and intense debate. The two senior pastors were on the committee and in the room as we explained what needed to be done. Some in the room never agreed with the cuts and I don't think they ever forgave a few of us for what we said and how we voted. To this day, I think we did the right thing. The alternative would have been far more painful in the long run. Had we not spoken out, however, I think that the other view would have carried the day. There were several people on the committee who weren't comfortable with having a hand in such matters and who needed a nudge to vote in our direction. When they saw a few of us willing to say what needed to be said, it made them willing to quietly vote what they felt, but had fought against accepting. Once a few people made the effort to speak up and take charge, the momentum began.

Taking Action

- Do you normally speak your opinion freely or try to stay quiet during debates and divisive situations? What drives you to that response?

- Have you ever witnessed the tide shift toward one solution over the alternatives after someone forcefully made a case? Why did it work?

- When you consider who you want involved in your next tough decision, would you rather have someone who actively tries to drive a solution or someone who will stay quiet and defer to others?

- It can be very uncomfortable to speak up and take charge. Prepare yourself ahead of time and commit to doing it. Otherwise, it will be too easy to back down when the time comes. Stick to your guns.

- Can you think of a time that you did not speak up when you had the chance and then later regretted it?

Chapter 21
Stay in Shape

Over the years, you will be absolutely inundated by information touting some way to get in shape and be healthier. Personally, I think the best policy is to get in shape when you are young and then stay that way. When my kids were little, my wife and I encouraged them to walk, run, swim, and generally be active. As with anything in life, once you get yourself into a regular habit of some sort, it is hard to break it. The same thing happens whether you are in shape or out of shape. Once in shape, it is easy to keep yourself in shape. Once you are out of shape, it is difficult to get back into a habit of exercise and very easy to remain out of shape.

Certainly there are health benefits to staying in good physical condition, but that was never my main motivation. It is more difficult to stick with an exercise routine if the only motivation is a vague promise of a longer and healthier life down the road. My motivation was much more immediate. I genuinely liked exercise and looked forward to it. More important, I was rewarded immediately by how good it made me feel. The vague promise of a longer and healthier life in the future was just an added bonus.

Ironically, I have found that exercising and staying in shape actually helps me have more energy, not less. According to what I have read and heard, this is true for many people. People who don't exercise often have the mistaken impression that it drains energy and that they can't afford to lose that energy if they are tired and struggling through their days. That is a false premise. Whenever I exercise and burn calories, it fires up both my body and my mind. I actually have more energy than I started with, and can accomplish more, not less. The idea that energy is a zero sum game just isn't valid.

There are times when I really don't feel like exercising because I am very tired or I don't feel well. Almost every time I force myself to exercise in such circumstances, I feel better almost immediately and it carries forward for a day or more. Every now and then, especially if I am sick, exercise won't work its magic for me. In those cases, I know I am truly sick and need to take it easy for a couple days. However, exercising to get myself through a funk works far more often than not.

As with anything, keeping in shape is a matter of how you set your priorities. You absolutely can find time to exercise if you try. In fact, once you are in shape, it is hard to imagine not working out regularly. Since the exercise will make you more effective and make you feel better, of course you are able to find time to do it.

When I was in college, people sometimes thought I was crazy to be going to the gym, playing soccer or racquetball the day before exams. I knew that by taking a break to exercise I'd be better off, both mentally and physically. I actually couldn't afford to skip it. The key here is that I didn't "spend" time exercising; I "invested" it. By taking a break and returning with an increased level of energy and focus, my average hourly output over the day was higher than if I hadn't taken the break. In fact, even while exercising, it is possible to get some study benefits. You can run through topics in your mind and work through the problems you are stuck on. It isn't really a situation of zero productivity. In fact, even today, when I am faced with a difficult problem related to work or my home life, I will take a break to exercise and think through the problems during the exercise. I often have my breakthroughs that way.

Exercise helps relieve stress for me in a big way. If it does the same for you, you'll probably also develop a strong drive to stick to an exercise regimen. I don't know how people I work with can handle the stress without the outlet of exercise to help relieve it.

A Few Examples from My Past

The momentum of being in shape is real. From time to time, I get injured and have to take time off exercise. By the end of four, six, or eight weeks of sitting around, I feel very out of shape and I have less energy. Given that my exercise time has been filled with other activities for a few weeks, I also can't remember how I used to find the time to exercise. It is amazing how quickly the time that had been used for exercise can be filled up with other activities. Initially, it can be hard to get back to a habit of exercise. However, after the great feeling I get following my first workout, I will be right back into it and never look back. It takes some effort and discipline to rebuild the habit, but it is worth it. Being in shape will improve both your mental and physical health for your whole life.

As I write this, I am in the middle of a huge reality check. I hurt my calf seven months ago and haven't been able to run since. I've gotten some exercise in, using stationary bikes and ellipticals, but not nearly as intense as usual and I feel like I am in very bad shape. In fact, I am probably in the worst condition I've been in since a big injury in college. I actually put an inch on my waist for the first time since college these past few months and my pants are tight. It is driving me crazy. Forty plus years of taking care of myself and one period of a few months off has shown me the difference. This is why it is important to stick to it. If you slip, you'll start down a bad path. Just like a home that isn't cleaned will quickly get dirty and fall into disrepair, so will your body. After decades of care and effort, I was impacted in a few short months.

I'd like to provide a specific example of how exercise doesn't need to take away from your daily tasks, even as you are taking time to do it. I often compile a list of issues and problems that I have to think through and that require some dedicated time and focus to resolve. From a work perspective, it might be how to structure a proposal or best persuade my coworkers to agree to a plan I am developing. I gather my general thoughts and review them before exercising. Whether I am running or biking, or doing something else, I use the time I am exercising to think through the problems. It is some good, uninterrupted time and I actually find it to be quite productive. Sitting at my desk, I would be interrupted by phone calls, email, or other tasks.

While running, I can focus intently without distractions of any kind. In this way, exercise sessions are actually critical parts of my work productivity. It isn't just an increased energy level later. I actually make use of my exercise time to get real work done. My exercise sessions are usually after or before work, not during work hours, but that doesn't really matter as the process works the same way. The combination of exercise and thinking through problems is powerful and one that many people don't recognize. Once you see it work for you, you'll embrace it as a critical part of your routine.

Exercise and staying in shape will pay off for you, I promise. I hope you are as naturally inclined toward and attracted to exercise as I am. If that's the case, staying in shape won't be a big effort for you anymore than it was for me. If you are a person to whom exercise doesn't come naturally, I hope that you can motivate yourself to do it anyway. Consider joining a class or other group activity to help you stick with it. Get your momentum going and maintain it. You'll be better for it.

Taking Action

- Do you currently exercise regularly? If so, keep it up. If not, get motivated by researching the benefits and then give it a try.

- Do you purposely exercise as a way to relax and think through problems? If not, try it. Often, the best time to exercise is when you least want to.

- Do you make a point to schedule your exercise time to ensure you make it happen? It is easy to have time pass and miss your window if you don't schedule the time and stick to it.

- Do you need extra motivation? Join an exercise class or start a formal program. It will give you an external push to keep going.

- Make a point to monitor your fatigue and stress levels before and after exercise. It will help you prove to yourself that exercise actually boosts your energy level, rather than depleting it.

Part Four

Resisting Pressure and Overcoming Adversity

Chapter 22
Getting Hurt

One thing that you'll experience in life is getting hurt—hurt emotionally, not physically, though you'll certainly have your share of physical injuries, too. In a perfect world, you'd never experience anything bad. In the real world, you won't be so lucky. All you can hope for is that you don't have more than your fair share of pain during your life. Some people just seem to have bad luck and have many horrible experiences. If you are not one of them, be thankful. If you are one of them, you'll need to find a way to deal with it.

Some of the first times you'll be hurt will likely be during school. Kids have a way of being very mean to one another. It gets even worse during the teen years. No one escapes growing up without being teased about something. It could be your hair, an outfit, or something you said, but eventually you will probably feel the wrath of multiple kids teasing you and just not letting it go. You could end up crying, feeling humiliated, or both. How you respond will partially determine how often it happens again.

One of the worst ways to respond to teasing is to show how much it bothers you. That will just encourage the people to do it again. After all, the point of teasing is to get a reaction from the victim. By ignoring it as best you can and getting away from the situation quickly, you keep the perpetrators' enjoyment to a minimum. Hopefully, they'll move on and find a different target. As discussed elsewhere in the book, make every effort not to be a part of the crowd doing the teasing. If you're tempted to take part, just think about how bad you felt when you were on the receiving end, or how you'd feel if someone in your family was getting the same treatment. Plus, teasing other people is just the wrong thing to do.

Another way you'll be hurt is when a friend has betrayed you or when someone ends a romantic relationship with you that you wanted to continue. This is a different type of hurt and can be one of the worst. Not many things feel worse than the feeling of rejection from someone you care about. It is almost certain you'll experience both of these scenarios during your life, and probably even before you're out of high school. You can't do much about it except let time pass. When you're freshly hurt, it will feel very bad and you'll think that you'll never feel good again. It is genuinely true that as time passes, you'll recover. Just as cuts and scrapes heal, so will your feelings. Of course, the worse the injury, the longer it can take. If something really upsetting happens, you may measure your recovery in weeks or months rather than days.

There will also be times that you cannot avoid hurting someone else. Perhaps you are in a relationship and it isn't working for you anymore. Even though you'll hurt the other person, it is better to be honest and break it off. However, you need to be sensitive to the other person's feelings. If someone is attached to you, and doesn't see the breakup coming, it can hurt them very badly. Do your best to be kind and to understand that their reaction, in the short term, can be a bit extreme, unusual, or even nasty. Allow the other person to vent their pain in whatever way they need to without letting it get to you. The last thing you want to do is to be drawn into a nasty argument where you both leave with a bad taste in your mouth. It is better to leave things on a positive note so that you can both move on more easily.

One final pain you'll experience will be the pain of loss when someone close to you dies. Given that everyone dies, this is an unavoidable part of life. Unless something very unusual happens, you'll live to see each of your grandparents die. You'll see your mom and dad die. In families with multiple children, some will see their siblings die. The worst pain is felt when one of the people closest to you passes away.

You can't do much to make the grieving process easier. You're going to experience it and it will be tough. The best you can do is to keep a perspective that pain and loss is part of life. You'll have to remind yourself that eventually you'll feel better, even if you can't really believe it at the time. As time passes, you'll heal.

A Few Examples from My Past

In college I had a girlfriend I was fond of. I used to have a reasonable number of dates, but rarely reached the "official girlfriend" point. If I wasn't very fond of somebody, I didn't waste my time or theirs. It always seemed odd to me that other people I knew would "give things a chance" for an extended period. I was either in or out when it came to a relationship. If I didn't feel a relationship was right at the outset, I didn't expect my opinion to change after a few more dates.

Since it was unusual for me to have an official girlfriend, whenever I reached that point it meant I was very, very fond of the person. One time I was falling hard for a particular girl and I was certainly looking forward to a long-lasting relationship, but things didn't go according to my plan. After a number of months, she blindsided me when she broke up with me. I hadn't seen the signs, so it felt like it came out of nowhere. I was incredibly hurt.

I remember being so upset that I needed to get out of town and into my comfort zone. I drove home for the weekend to stay with my parents. It was one of the only times I went home just for a weekend when I was in college. My parents knew what had happened, but didn't push me to reveal much. They just let me hang out, eat some food I liked, and be home. It really did help and I so appreciated being able to go home to them like that. If you ever have a similar need, I hope that you'll be comfortable going home to your parents, too. I also hope your parents will be as helpful to you as my parents were to me.

Another occasion I remember relates to a good friend in high school. We went to different schools, but had become great friends while playing on a soccer team together. We hung out almost every weekend for at least a year. All of a sudden, he stopped wanting to hang out. It hurt pretty badly because I considered him one of my very best friends. He never really offered any explanation. We hadn't had a fight or anything else that would explain the sudden change. To this day, I'm not sure what the deal was, but sometimes life is a mystery.

As you get older, you can expect to drift apart from some of your friends, too. People do change, especially as they grow up. You can expect a shift with some of the people you are close to over time. It won't make it easier when you part ways with a friend, but when it happens, if you can recognize that you aren't alone in your experience, it will help keep it in perspective.

Probably the worst pain I ever felt was when my mother died with no warning whatsoever. She had a sudden brain hemorrhage on Christmas Eve and died instantly. She had been in very good health and her death was totally unexpected. Everyone in the family was devastated. As bad as it hit me, I can barely imagine how hard it hit my father. I honestly didn't realize how bad something could hurt and upset me until that experience. I'm not usually a highly emotional person. If anything, sometimes I worry that I am not emotional enough, with my logical brain and approach to life. However, the one good thing that came out of that experience was that I realized that I do have deep, real emotions, even if they don't come out very often.

It took me a long time to stop feeling sad about losing my mom. I dread going through it again with my dad, but that event is just another part of life I'll have to deal with. You'll have similar experiences, too. The key to getting through those times is accepting them as an unavoidable and necessary part of life. The experiences will be difficult, but you can get through them.

Taking Action

- Have you ever been hurt badly? How did you handle the pain you experienced? Did you learn anything from it?

- Have you ever hurt someone else? What did you do to try and soften the blow? Could you have done better?

- Do you know anyone who has had a large amount of pain in his or her life? Are you sensitive to the fact that it can impact the way he or she interacts with others, including you?

- Have you seen someone handle emotional pain in a very poor way? What can you do differently if you ever end up in the same situation?

- Given that people can pass away at any time, are you focused on keeping your relationships with those you love on a positive note?

Chapter 23
Setting Sexual Boundaries

This is a rather uncomfortable topic to write about and it is likely uncomfortable for you to read, but it is important. The bottom line is that boys are pigs. Many boys will do anything to get some "action" from a girl. The rest manage to resist their pig tendencies successfully. In recent times, it seems that many girls are as bad as boys. It isn't a good way to be. You should be taking any sexual interactions, and especially "big" sexual interactions, very seriously. It isn't a game. It can lead to a damaged reputation, disease, or a poorly-timed baby. The idea that sexual activities are all fun and games isn't true, even though many people act as though it is.

You need to decide what you want to do, with whom, and when. I hope you'll make good decisions and postpone most sexual activities until you are old enough to be in a mature, committed, loving relationship. Ideally you will wait until you are married. Today, there is still a very large portion of society that holds a strong belief that people should be married before having sex. What you see on TV or read doesn't reflect the size of the segment of the population that holds these views. You can't assume that what is typical and normal in the media is typical and normal in our population. Very few people truly believe that having a carefree attitude about sex is the best way to live, even if they are choosing to live that way. It doesn't matter what I say here or what anyone else says to you, you'll make your own decisions about how you'll handle things. Regardless of your approach to sexual activities, think through what your limits are, set them firmly in your mind, and stand by them when the time comes.

The last thing you want is to be alone with someone in a setting where sexual activity would be possible without some clear boundaries in your head. You may have had a great date and before you know it, you are having a make-out session with someone. After it starts, you will have to apply your limits on how far you'll go. If you don't have clear boundaries in your head before you get into such a situation, you'll almost certainly go further than you would have wanted to if asked ahead of time.

The heat of the moment can make your decision-making capabilities substandard to say the least. Add alcohol to the mix and your chance of making poor decisions goes up immensely. If your physical and emotional feelings are going crazy without a firm boundary drawn in your mind, your mind may very well lose. Many people still slip up and go further than they want even with a firm boundary set in their mind ahead of time. The bottom line is that you can't afford not to have boundaries firmly set and to remind yourself of them regularly. Without those boundaries, you are putting yourself at risk.

If you are a male, please try to control your pig instincts. Every guy has them. Some of the boys that you will know will be pure pigs. They won't respect girls. They'll view them just as a conquest to pursue. They'll treat them poorly. They'll lie to them. They'll just act like pigs. Do better than that.

When you find yourself thinking in ways that can be considered "piggish," or being influenced by others in that direction, take a step back and ground yourself again. I was appalled by the actions and attitudes of many of the boys I knew.

Many of those who appalled me were decent guys, but they started down a bad path. Once they started treating girls badly and not respecting them, they just kept getting worse and worse. The best way to bring yourself back to earth is to ask yourself some questions. For example: "How would I feel if someone said that about my mom or sister? How would I feel if someone acted that way towards my mom or sister? How would I feel if someone thought that way about my mom or sister?"

If you find your answer to those questions disturbing, adjust your mindset. Remind yourself that any girl you are at risk of treating in a way that made you ask those questions could be someone's sister, will probably be someone's mom one day, and does have a dad who would be upset with you as well.

If you are a female, you need to be very alert in today's environment. It just isn't as safe as it used to be. Girls get taken advantage of frequently. The best way to ensure your safety is to look out for yourself. You also need to be strong and resist pressure from boys if they are pushing you to do more things sexually than you are comfortable with. I don't know a single boy who would actually break up with a girl he really, truly liked just because of what she won't do physically. Any boy who says, "If you really loved me. . . ." doesn't love you. I saw boys boast about how they guilt-tripped girls to get them to go further than the girls really wanted to go.

It seems that with today's youth, many girls are as aggressive sexually as boys. While I am not sure how this trend came to be, I am sure that it isn't a good one. When I was young, the girls served as a voice of reason and a sanity check. However unfairly, they often served as the speed limit sign that many boys weren't willing to be. If nobody is playing that role in a situation, then the tendency is to keep on going at full speed. It is up to each individual to firmly establish their own limit and stick to it. As a girl, you'll need to set your boundaries and be prepared to defend them diligently.

Another risk you'll face is that some boys and girls will only too happily tell all their friends about what happened, possibly even posting details on a social media site. It can cause a lot of embarrassment. Even if you only tell your closest friends what happened, this assumes your friends can be trusted to keep your confidence. However, those friends may violate your trust and say something you'd not want. The result is the same, with a lot of people knowing what you did, whether you like it or not.

With the proliferation of smartphones and social media, you might have an even harder time keeping your indiscretion private. When you kiss that person at the party, somebody just might snap a picture and post it on the Internet. Or, they might send a message to a friend telling them about it. Your actions can go very public, very quickly. Your actions are no longer just a rumor that is soon forgotten. Today, the details can be cemented in pictures and writing forever. The best way to avoid this is to know what you're willing to do before you are in a situation where you need to decide, and be careful to keep your private life private. The key is for you to set your sexual boundaries up front, review them regularly, and stick to them.

A Few Examples from My Past

Having known guys who just viewed girls as a conquest to be made, I think I was a good judge of whether or not guys were legitimately interested in a girl, or just trying to score. One time my sister was asked out by a boy from our neighborhood. I had met him a few times, and had a clear impression that he was an utter pig. I told my sister that the guy was trouble and was after one thing, but she didn't believe me. I told her that I'd bet he'd start pressuring her after 2 or 3 dates and that she'd probably get dumped within a month or so if she hadn't complied with his desires. She thought I was crazy. Sure enough, however, I hit it on the head. She admitted that I was dead on. He dumped her after about a month, when it became clear she wasn't going to be an easy score. Luckily, my sister had set firm boundaries and stuck to them.

On another front, I saw many occasions where someone was out with friends, had a bit too much to drink, and ended up fooling around with someone more than they should have. Sometimes, it was as simple as kissing someone that they didn't know well, and certainly weren't in a relationship with. Other times, it involved more serious activities in private. The point is that I saw many people immediately regret and be embarrassed by their actions. This is why it is important to have firm boundaries in your mind before you get into such a situation. It will help you put the brakes on before you go too far. You can't regret doing something you didn't do.

Taking Action

- Have you established firm boundaries in terms of how far you'll go sexually? If not, set some now to protect yourself.

- Do you put yourself into situations where you are at risk? If so, how can you make some changes to your habits to stop doing that?

- Have you asked friends to remind you of your limits if it appears that you may be tested? Having some backup is always a good thing.

- Do you ever stop to ask yourself if the way you are treating and thinking about people of the opposite sex is how you'd like people to think of you, or your siblings, or your parents?

- Are you choosing friends who share your limits, or do you feel pressure to "loosen up?" If the latter, reconsider your choice of friends.

Chapter 24
Drugs and Drinking

As you move through your teen years, drugs and alcohol will be something you'll start dealing with. Unfortunately, I don't think it is possible to make it out of high school without coming across drugs and alcohol in some way. The decisions you make when faced with these substances can have a very large impact on who you become and what future you will have. Actions you take while under the influence of drugs or alcohol have the potential to hurt or kill others, as well as yourself. Those actions also have the potential to ruin your life by generating a permanent criminal record for you.

Let's start with the physical dangers. Many drugs are highly addictive and very bad for your body. Crystal Meth, for example, will addict you quickly, and rot your teeth away if you use it with any regularity. Addiction is a horrible thing and many people never escape from it. They either end up dead, in jail, or living a meaningless and miserable life. Nobody plans to get addicted to drugs or alcohol, but by the time you realize that you're getting addicted, it can be too late.

Another set of physical dangers come from situations you may find yourself in. You, or the friend transporting you, might wind up driving under the influence, which can lead to injury or death. You could pass out and be taken advantage of sexually. You can get into a bad situation where somebody beats you up (or worse). Being heavily intoxicated can lead to all sorts of dangerous situations. Intoxication will also make you handle those situations much more poorly than you would otherwise.

I hope that you'll reject drugs outright throughout your life. There really isn't much good that can come out of using drugs. The laws against drugs are strict and firmly in place. One arrest record related to drugs can ruin your chances at many jobs later in life. It just isn't worth that risk. Similarly, having a DUI (driving under the influence) arrest can derail many future opportunities. Most companies today run background checks on perspective employees, and any arrest record will show up. These days, a drunk or drugged driving conviction is considered a major sign of irresponsibility and many employers will pass on you if your record shows one.

Underage drinking can also lead to an arrest. Eventually, you'll be legally allowed to drink alcohol. Regardless of your age, if you're going to drink, very clearly set your limits up front. Once you start drinking, it is very easy to get sucked into drinking more than you planned. This is especially true when you're with a group who is partying and encouraging it. Consequently, drinking and sex require similar approaches. Make a deal with yourself beforehand about exactly how much you will and won't drink, then force yourself to stick to that plan. Self-control drops rapidly as you start drinking, and it only gets worse the more you drink. Don't underestimate the stupid things you may do. It is better to avoid the situation by setting limits in advance.

I know you won't want to think about all the bad things that can happen years down the road when you are a teenager or young adult and just want to have fun. I know I didn't. I was lucky that I grew up in a time where a few stupid mistakes would be more easily forgotten. There was no Facebook, no cell phones to take a picture of a stupid action, and more willingness for authorities to let kids off the hook if they weren't repeat offenders. Unfortunately, you don't have those luxuries. Just attending one big party and getting caught with a beer in your hand can reverberate far into your future. Focus on making good decisions from the very beginning. If you make some of the same mistakes I made, you'll suffer much more for them in today's world than I did years ago.

A Few Examples from My Past

I have seen friends ruin their lives with alcohol or drugs. I'll tell you three stories, starting with the least disturbing. My first example relates to the fact that I knew a lot of people in college who drank way too much and way too often. They would party so much that they didn't keep their grades up. Instead of studying, they'd go to a party. When test time came, they were too tired from being out all night to perform well. As a result, I saw many people flunk out. It seemed so stupid to flunk out and give up a bright future just for a few nights of fun, but many people did it.

Before one guy I knew was able to officially flunk out (he was on academic probation), he got very drunk one night. Somehow, he ended up breaking the window of a business downtown. He was caught and charges were pressed. He ended up with a criminal record, in addition to being expelled from the university when he was only a freshman. What a change of life options and outlook he had during that partial school year. No longer a new freshman with a bright future ahead, he went back home with no degree and a criminal record. I don't know what happened to him, but I can't imagine that things turned out nearly as well as he and his family had hoped when he first arrived at college. I'd hate to see something like that happen to you.

The second example involves marijuana. Many people consider pot totally safe and harmless. No matter what anybody says, I am certain that it can become mentally addictive, given what I have seen. I knew a number of people in college who got sucked into smoking pot on a daily basis. The result of all that pot smoking was a complete loss of motivation. I saw pot smokers' grades plummet. I also saw many of them become totally unreliable people. The term back then for such people was "stoner" or "pothead." People with that label were expected to be a bit slow in their speech and movement, unable to be counted on for anything important, and unconcerned with their progress in school. Some people I knew even went so far as to become "wake and bakes," meaning that they literally kept pot by their alarm clock so that they could smoke as soon as the alarm went off. Then, from there, they would continue to smoke all day long. What a waste.

One gentleman I knew living this way was complaining one night about how his parents didn't trust him and his grades were horrid. He admitted that all his pot smoking was having an impact. I challenged him—if he was truly concerned, he needed to quit smoking. I told him that I wouldn't listen to him whine about it as long as he kept smoking. He made a commitment to stop smoking the next day and he actually stuck to it. He clearly knew before we talked that it was the right option for him. I think our discussion served as the final kick he needed to take action.

The next semester he got all A's and B's for the first time. Unfortunately, some of his pot-smoking friends didn't take kindly to his change of lifestyle. Over the summer, they sucked him back into smoking pot. Once he started smoking again, he didn't stop. His grades were back in trouble in the fall and once again, his parents were unhappy. While he managed to finish school, he certainly didn't live up to his potential. His use of pot was far from harmless and I wonder how it has impacted his life if he continued in the same fashion after graduation, which seems likely.

My last example ends very badly. One person I knew in college was a heavy drug user. He didn't just use pot, but other things, like LSD, on a regular basis. I had no indication of this when I met him, but quickly found out. He believed the claims that drugs are dangerous and bad for people were just silly. He was certain LSD and other drugs were harmless and safe to use.

He genuinely thought I was a loser for not seeing things his way and joining him in using drugs. For a long time, unlike many, he was actually able to pull off his drug use with little noticeable impact.

A few years after I graduated, I got a note from a mutual friend. It seems my friend's drug use continued after college, and he continued to use a wider variety of drugs. Eventually, he got into heroin. One day, when he was in his late twenties, he was found dead from a heroin overdose in his bathroom. Anytime I hear people talk about how drugs are harmless and safe in small doses, I think of him. I knew him fairly well and he was a decent guy. However, those drugs, that he seemed to use without harm for many years, eventually caught up with him. He thought drugs were harmless and fun, but he learned in the hardest way possible that he was wrong.

I hope that you stay away from drugs so that you don't become someone with a similar story. I am against drugs, not to be old-fashioned or because I am a "goody-goody." I am against them because I have witnessed firsthand how drugs can lead people to mess up, or even end their lives.

Taking Action

- Have you committed to yourself to avoiding drugs? If not, do it. Be committed before you ever come across them.

- If you choose to drink, make sure to establish your limits up front before having a single drop.

- Will you commit to sticking to your limits even at the height of a great party with friends encouraging you to keep drinking? This will be your true test.

- Have you seen someone suffer from bad decisions they made when using drugs or alcohol?

- Have you done research to learn about the impacts addiction can have on your body, mind, and spirit? Disturbing true-life stories abound.

Chapter 25
Cheating

Wherever rules or agreements are in place, there are always people that will take advantage of the rules or even just ignore them. One of the most common ways that kids break the rules is by cheating in school. Given the amount of time spent in school, cheating on homework or tests easily ranks as one of the most common types of cheating that kids engage in. I define cheating as any action taken outside of the established boundaries that enables you or another person to perform better at a task than is deserved.

I wish I could tell you that cheating is an issue that only impacts kids, but many grown-ups cheat, too. Once a person falls into a pattern of cheating, it can be hard to break that pattern. This means that it is important for you to resist getting drawn into cheating when you are young. As with many bad habits, it is much easier to stay away from cheating from the beginning, than to pull yourself away from it after you've adopted the habit. Not only does cheating compromise your integrity, it taints any achievements you attain.

When I was in high school, cheating was somewhat common. I have heard that it is worse today. Many kids just didn't have any issue with cheating. They simply accepted it as something you did if you thought you could get away with it. Of course, you won't always get away with it. When you are caught, it can carry serious consequences, not just to your grades, but to your reputation.

If you're caught cheating today you can expect to get a 0 percent on the specific test or assignment—that's if you don't flunk the class entirely. Having a single 'F' on your record is enough to ruin your chances of getting into a good college or graduate school. It is also enough to bring a solid grade point average down to something much less impressive. The risks just aren't worth the benefits. It is far better to miss a few questions than to cheat and risk losing credit for all of the questions.

There were kids in school with me who were known to be big into cheating. This wasn't viewed as a positive trait, even though many kids didn't seem to care much that others cheated. However, as time passed, the cheaters were viewed less positively by most people except those cheating right along with them. I think people just have a hard time trusting someone at all if they know the person can't be trusted to do their schoolwork honestly.

Cheating isn't limited to school. People are regularly found to have cheated on everything from sports to board games. In fact, professional athletes have been caught violating rules or using drugs in order to achieve more than they were able to achieve by following the rules. Any of these types of cheating will compromise your reputation. Unless you have no compass for right and wrong, I can't imagine that cheating won't make you feel worse about yourself. You'll know inside that you cheated and didn't deserve your success.

Make the decision to keep cheating out of your life; succeed or fail on your own merits. There are times when you may be disappointed by how you finish, and that's okay. You can't win every time, but a victory is hollow and fake if it is only achieved through cheating. If others think cheating is acceptable, that's their business. You need to be better than that.

A Few Examples from My Past

I have never forgotten what happened during an eighth grade math test. I was very good in math and had no trouble getting A's in my class. There was a test with an extra credit question and the question totally stumped me. I walked to the teacher's desk to ask her to clarify what she was looking for. A friend of mine heard me ask and realized that I was struggling with the question. As I walked back to my desk, my friend got my attention and pointed to what he had written down on his paper and I saw the answer. For some reason, I decided to go ahead and put that answer down on my paper. I had not intended to cheat that day, but somehow allowed myself to do it once I saw the answer.

The next day the teacher called me over. She told me that she found it quite suspicious that I was stumped when I asked her the question and then got the right answer in the final few minutes of the test. She asked me if I had cheated. I felt horrible and admitted what had happened. She told me she was very disappointed. I got lucky because she decided my only punishment would be to miss that specific question instead of something more serious. I think the only reason she was that easy on me is because she knew I didn't usually cheat and she could tell I felt badly.

The point of the story is that you have to be on guard at all times. I had no intention of cheating, no history of cheating, and no need to cheat, yet somehow ending up doing so in the spur of the moment. Keep focused on what your values are so that when you are tested the way I was tested, you will do better than I did in my eighth-grade math class.

One last example relates to high school. As I mentioned, there were classmates who cheated as much as they could get away with. In many cases, it wasn't that they were unable to do the work, but just an easy way out. Believe it or not, cheating was also somewhat "cool" to some kids. I suppose this was because it showed that you were willing to rebel against the school and teachers. It also was a way to bond with fellow cheaters.

Some of the friends I had from the soccer team cheated quite a bit and they were in classes with me. I remember having people ask me if they could copy from my test paper. The way this would typically be achieved is that person #1 would move his or her paper over to the side of his or her desk so that person #2 could glance at it. People wouldn't typically copy all the answers from someone else, but try to copy just a couple that they were stuck on.

I wish that I could say that I never let anyone look at my paper, but I did do it a few times. I'm not sure why I made that decision. I recall a few times a friend asked me to let him see my paper before a test and I would do it. I justified it as a part of being a good friend. I also gave into the pressure of not being viewed as an uptight goody-goody by saying no. The problem is that after you've let someone copy a few answers from your paper once, it seems a lot easier to let someone copy the next time. I regretted the decision to let people cheat from me at the time and still do to this day. I didn't need to do it and it exposed me to some big risks that I didn't need.

Realizing my error, I made a vow before I went to college that I would never take part in any cheating of any type again. I am proud to say that I stuck to that vow. Not one time, through college and graduate school, did I cheat in any way or facilitate others cheating in any way. Part of what helped me stick to this decision was the fact that I became aware that colleges have "Honor Codes" that set guidelines for what is acceptable. After reading and thinking about my school's honor code, I decided that it was right. It reinforced my stance.

The above point is worth extra attention. By reading an honor code, it helped me reset my attitude and keep myself in line. It is a good idea to think regularly about what you believe in. It is also a good idea to read books or discuss important moral topics on a regular basis. By focusing your attention on these topics, it helps to remind you what's important to you and keeps you from slowly straying.

I think this is one of the main benefits of attending church. Churches provide an environment that always leads you to think about what is right and wrong. That influence can really help to keep you on the right path in life. I hope that this book can serve a similar role in your life by encouraging you to review many of the attitudes you have and the decisions you are making.

Taking Action

- Have you ever cheated? If so, what made you do it?

- If you agree that cheating is not the right thing to do, why not vow to live a life free of cheating today?

- What pressures have you had from others to cheat? How have you handled it in the past? How might you handle it in the future?

- What do you think of public figures, such as athletes, who have been caught cheating? Would you like others to think the same of you?

- What justifications do you hear people use for cheating? What are some rebuttals you can make to those justifications?

Chapter 26
Playing Politics

You'll be amazed at how much time and energy people waste "playing politics." People play political games at work, at school, at church . . . just about anywhere that people interact on a regular basis. Political games seem to be a fact of life for human society. For the most part, I consider the energy spent on politics an utter waste of time. I do not consider using common sense and following reasonable protocols to be politics. I am talking about taking or not taking actions for purely political purposes.

For example, being respectful of everyone at work is simply the right thing to do. It is also true that the further up the chain a person is from you, the more careful you need to be not to needlessly upset them. If a person can fire you for a misunderstanding, you have to be smart and stay on your toes. Being smart about how you behave and ensuring you are respectful is very different from kissing up or trying to make yourself look good at the expense of others. That crosses the line into playing politics.

The worst thing to do is to get pulled into petty politics. Petty politics includes things like gossiping about people's personal lives behind their backs, or trying to make someone look bad for your benefit. There are people who are masterful at playing politics. Some people actually get quite far in life through their political maneuvers. In most cases, however, others don't respect the people who succeed this way. I think it would be horrible to be viewed as having a position because of who you know, or who owed you a favor, instead of having earned it. When his or her benefactor moves on, a person like this is often quickly disposed of by those who come into power next.

Many people will tell you that you have to play politics to get ahead. I don't believe that. I believe you have to be smart about what you say and do. That is not the same as playing politics in the negative sense of the word. You really don't need to play politics to get ahead. Instead, be honest, do good work, and follow through on your word. If you do those things, you'll get along better than most of the people that do play politics.

Understand, there will be occasions where someone playing politics will beat you out of something. I am not saying you will win every battle by steering clear of politics. I am saying, however, that you can win the war. Even in those cases where you get frustrated because a political person beats you, you can feel good and proud that if you do win the next round, you'll have won playing fair and square. While people more focused on politics than performing and adding value sometimes do make it to the top, most do not.

I believe the key to success, while staying out of politics, is to be clearly uninterested in playing. People will notice that you aren't playing. Those who don't like playing politics will respect and appreciate you for it. Those that do play politics will know where you are coming from and that you aren't plotting a hidden attack on them. Since you aren't a threat, they'll usually leave you alone. Occasionally, one of the political folks will get you. That's life. Just be extra cautious going forward with that person, just as you would with anyone else you know you can't trust.

I visualize a common movie scene when thinking of how I try to position myself politically. In movies there will sometimes be a huge fight in a bar or restaurant with almost everyone involved. There will be one guy, however, that just sits in his seat and sips his drink while mayhem erupts around him. He typically doesn't get hit or drawn into the fight because everyone has bigger problems to worry about. After the fight, everyone else has to deal with their injuries, but the guy who stayed out of it just continues to enjoy himself as if nothing happened. I aim to be the guy who watches everyone else fighting it out around me. At the end of the big fight, I'll be refreshed, uninjured, and less stressed than anyone else. Better still, since I didn't enter the fight, nobody will consider me a part of the "other team" so I haven't created any new enemies.

A Few Examples from My Past

At one point in my career, I was working for a large company. Over time, I learned that there were politics being played at a deeper level than I initially realized. I was just plain oblivious to some of it, which I found disconcerting. How had I missed seeing what was going on? As a result, I questioned whether I would be able to navigate such an environment, given my style of avoiding the political battles.

Soon after my realization, I had a conversation about an idea that a co-worker brought to me that would require cooperation across a couple of teams. After meeting with a few people, I expressed my willingness to help. After the meeting, the co-worker pulled me aside. He said it was refreshing to work with me, since I played things straight up and was genuinely interested in doing the right thing for the company, as opposed to just looking for ways to advance my own agenda.

I thought it was a shame that he felt such behavior was a rare exception, but clearly, my style and approach was working in that environment after all. A few other people expressed similar views over time and I found myself able to make more allies and get more initiatives pushed forward in the company than many who were very adept at politics. I stuck to my positions and stayed out of the political games as much as I could.

On another occasion, a former co-worker served as a reference for me when I was interviewing for a job. He was asked what I was like to work with. I was told that his comment stressed the point that you always knew what you were getting with me. He said that I'd act the same when talking to a secretary as when talking to a CEO. That commentary really helped me with my potential employer and I think it was one of the nicest things I've ever heard said about me. I don't know what I would value much more than someone realizing that I simply played things straight and didn't put on a bunch of different personas based on who I was talking to and what I thought they wanted to hear. To have someone recognize my approach and use it as part of a recommendation made me very happy.

One last story is from high school. My junior year, I ran to be senior class treasurer. My opponent was a very popular cheerleader. I won. I think that a good part of the reason was the way I avoided playing politics and tried to be friendly with everyone. One minute I would be chatting in the hall with one of the big jocks, and the next, one of the big geeks from math class. My guess is that my opponent and I split the vote closely among the socially active crowd. I might even have lost if that was the only group voting. My secret weapon was that many of the kids who were outsiders, and certainly not part of the "in" crowd, had no issue with me. I am confident that I won a large part of the vote among such students. That was enough to get me the win. If I had played the typical high school politics of worrying every minute about who I was talking to and how it would be perceived, I might have lost that election.

If you can stick to your beliefs and avoid politics, I think you'll also be able to do well for yourself. In the short term, it won't always be obvious that it's working, but over time you will see the results and sleep better at night knowing you're playing it straight.

Taking Action

- Do you allow yourself to get pulled into politics more than you should? What can you do to avoid getting pulled in next time?

- Are you careful to treat everyone equally and with respect? If not, you could be hurting your reputation.

- Have you seen examples of people for whom playing politics backfires?

- If you examine your feelings, do you prefer to associate with people who play politics or with people who you can take at face value? Act like someone you'd prefer to associate with yourself.

- Are you willing to make a concerted effort to minimize the time and energy you put into political games? Commit to it and regularly assess if you are succeeding.

Chapter 27
Don't Just Follow the Crowd

It is surprising how much other people can influence our actions. Most people have a natural inclination to want to get along with others and prefer to avoid conflict unless it is required. As a result, when what you believe, or what you want to do, does not match up with those around you, you'll find yourself struggling with how to proceed. Do you go along with the crowd to avoid standing out and possibly being chastised as a result? Or do you stick to your initial position, regardless of the consequences? This is not an easy decision and the fact is that there will be times when each of those options will be the right decision.

In situations where a decision isn't very important, sometimes going along with the consensus is a good way to go. If a group of people can't agree on where to go for dinner, it isn't worth causing a conflict over a less desirable choice. If you are the roadblock or the one complaining frequently, people will eventually just dismiss you and your opinion. By strategically picking when you push back, and doing it infrequently, you can get people to listen when you do choose to push back. Let the things that are not important to you go in whatever direction they may so that when the time comes, you'll have the ability to influence the things that are important to you.

You won't always win when you push back, even on some things that are important to you. You can maximize your chances of successfully swaying opinion by picking your battles intelligently, but it won't work every time. The percentage of the time you'll win people over will depend, in part, on how much your view or plan diverges from the consensus. The more drastically different your opinion is, the less likely you'll prevail. These moments will require a gut check. It can be difficult to stand your ground when it is clear you won't win others over. It can be tempting to change your position, or simply defer to the group without changing your position. On matters where important principles are involved, however, think about who you are and what you stand for before you decide how to proceed.

There are many cases throughout history where people caved in and supported (or at least failed to resist) horrible positions. This has led to some dark times in the world. Two world wars began because people did not rise in large numbers against evil leaders and policies before it was too late. There are also examples of good people getting sucked into criminal enterprises because they didn't put their foot down as the ethics of the decisions being made around them slowly degraded. Look up the story of Enron for a terrific example of this. On the flip side, there are many situations when a few brave souls stood up for something that went against the common standard and ended up changing society for the better. Look up the story of Rosa Parks for an example of this.

You may find yourself in a position later in life where standing up for what you believe in might make you unpopular, cost you your job, or even put you at risk of persecution. The real test of your character will be whether you have the guts to stand up for what you believe in and accept the consequences. History is littered with people who said "If only I had done or said something earlier."

A Few Examples from My Past

In the business world, there can be a lot of pressure. I believe our business environment is currently unhealthy in the sense that Wall Street and the financial world only cares about the next quarterly results and end-of-year results for an organization. This creates immense pressure to produce those numbers. Worse, it encourages people to make decisions that maximize short-term results, even when it may do long-term harm. An executive can keep his job today and get a great bonus by making shortsighted decisions. If he's not acting ethically and isn't resisting the pressure of the crowd to post numbers each quarter, he has to hope he's moved on to a new role before the house of cards he builds from those short-term decisions comes crashing down. I hope these pressures will change, but you'll need to be prepared to deal with such an environment and you'll need to decide how far you're willing to go.

Early in my career, the division I worked in was struggling to make our yearly numbers. I knew there was pressure on my boss (and every other member of the leadership team) to come up with some extra revenue at the end of the year. I recall that we had a terrific Christmas party for the whole office. Afterward, I saw the head of the division corner a few members of his leadership team, including my boss, and tell them each how much revenue they had to "find" by the end of the week. It put a bad taste in my mouth because it was obvious that he just wanted a good number to report, whether the revenue was legitimate or not.

A couple days later, my boss confided in me about a problem. He had been directed to book some revenue for a client. Given the status of the project, the large amount of revenue requested was not legitimate, but my boss was asked to book the revenue anyway. This was clearly a move to make the numbers look better than they were. Under today's laws, booking such revenue would be much harder to do. Under the laws at the time, it just took a signature.

I told my boss that if I were him, I would not sign off on the revenue and expose myself to being accused of fraud later. After some thought, he decided to draft up the document for signature and then give it to the division manager. If that manager wanted to sign off on the revenue, that was his business, not that of my boss. He gave the document to the division manager who then signed and submitted it.

The division manager didn't last much longer in his role. I suspect his methods were uncovered. I am not sure that my boss and I should feel that good about ourselves either. We didn't book any revenue inappropriately and we didn't encourage anyone else to either. However, once we knew what he was doing, we should have challenged the division manager and taken the issue to his management. Neither of us had the stomach to do that for fear of losing our jobs. You could fairly accuse us of following the crowd and turning the other way on that occasion. I hope you are never in a similar situation and, unlike me, I hope you won't look back with regret about the way you handled it.

Another situation where I'd say I was only half right was in high school. A very heavy kid was teased all the time. I thought how he was treated was horrible. On several occasions, I was with people who teased him. I did not join in, and once or twice I told others to leave the kid alone. So, I did better than many, but I can't say that I did everything I could or should have done to defend the boy. Whenever I was around the teasing, I should have jumped in and told everyone to stop immediately. I didn't do that because I didn't want to cause trouble for myself. I got sucked into following the crowd more than going against it. At the time, I was proud of myself for not joining in. Looking back, I am embarrassed that the boy could reasonably have perceived me as taking part and sanctioning the teasing due to my silence, or my less than convincing suggestion that the others stop.

There have been times in my life where I didn't follow the crowd in any way and I did what was right without compromise. I think the examples illustrating my failures are more thought-provoking, however, which is why I chose to discuss them instead.

Taking Action

- Have you ever given in, followed the crowd, and later regretted it? What led to your decision and what led to your regret?

- Have you ever stood up for what you believe in even though you paid a price for doing so? How did you feel afterward?

- What beliefs do you hold dear enough that you would risk great harm in order to stand by them?

- Have there been situations where you have seen someone else's beliefs or principles tested? Did they stand their ground or cave to the pressure?

- Are you flexible about small issues so that people won't dismiss you as disagreeable? Pick your battles wisely so that you will have influence when you need it.

Chapter 28
What is Cool Now
Isn't Always Cool Later

As you enter junior high school and become a teenager, it suddenly seems very important to be seen as "cool." If you can't be seen as cool, you definitely don't want to be seen in any way as "un-cool." This is a seemingly natural and unavoidable part of growing up. Some people handle it better than others. They are not drawn as far astray by their natural tendencies.

One thing that has always struck me as odd is how what is viewed as cool seems to change with age. When you are an early teenager, "cool" is often highly associated with behavior that is off the wall. The person who is willing to do the most daring thing, the most obnoxious thing, or the craziest thing is the coolest. As an early teenager, you will be tempted to do all sorts of outrageous things just to keep up with your friends. As hard as it will be, control your urges as much as possible. A bunch of young teenagers can encourage each other to the point that they are really crossing the line. A few too many "I dare you to . . ."

rounds and the next thing you know, somebody is hurt or has gotten into big trouble all for the sake of trying to be cool.

This is still an issue as you get to be a late teen, but the focus will be less on being totally outrageous and more on acting in the ways that are considered cool, and acting that way with people who are considered cool. Behavior will often, but not always, be better moderated at this age. By the time you enter college, getting too outrageous starts to be frowned upon. By the end of college, you'll start to realize that being cool might not carry as much weight in the real world as you thought it did in your early years.

I mention this for three reasons. First, I am hoping that I can help you realize that you will feel the urge to be cool just like everyone else. Second, I also hope that you will be able to resist succumbing to the pressure to be cool to the point that it impacts you negatively. Third, if you read what I said, you'll realize that what is considered cool at one point in life often isn't considered cool later.

This last point is important. If I think back about who the coolest kids were in junior high, very few of them remained that way. Those who were willing to push the limits hard enough to be super cool in junior high often got sucked too deeply into risky behaviors and ended up in a ton of trouble in high school. They went from super cool to troublemaker. This did not happen all the time, but it did happen frequently.

Similarly, those who were the coolest in high school often weren't so cool a few years down the road. When people focus so much energy on trying to be cool, it seems they often let other areas, like academics, slip. Also, it is easy to develop a snobby attitude if you are viewed as cool and popular in high school. Within a few years of high school ending, people really don't have time for those who are snobby. Suddenly it isn't at all cool to have such an attitude.

What I'd like you to focus on as you grow up is being yourself. You certainly don't have to go out of your way to rebel against all of the behavioral and social norms of the day, but you certainly shouldn't blindly follow them either. It will be hard to imagine anyone or anything that is considered cool at any point in time ever being considered anything else. Trust me, it will happen. Don't jeopardize your long-term character, reputation, and future over trying to fit in today.

This is one lesson you'll need to focus on and remind yourself of on a regular basis. You will probably think I am dead wrong about my comments here at times. I can only ask that you trust that I am more right than you will think when you are young. Go ahead and try to be cool and fit in to some extent if you must, but think very carefully about how far you'll take the efforts. Ask yourself if what you are doing and how you are behaving and treating others is something you'll be proud of later. If you have any doubt, consider changing course.

A Few Examples from My Past

In junior high, some of the cool kids seemed to have amazingly exciting lives compared to me. Sometimes, they were even invited to high school parties—the ultimate stamp of coolness. They were known to do daring things that most of us would never have the nerve to do. They had boyfriends or girlfriends before the rest of us. That's part of what made them so cool. We all secretly wished we could do what they did.

I also recall watching through high school as almost all of the coolest kids from junior high slipped from view. Several got into drinking and drugs quite heavily. Some turned into juvenile delinquents who got into trouble with the law. A few managed to maintain their cool status, but there was a definite trend of shifting down the coolness scale for the coolest kids from junior high. I am convinced that it is partly because those who are willing to be so extreme in junior high either have problems at home or don't have appropriate impulse controls. In junior high their actions seem daring, exciting, and quite cool. Later on, much of the behavior seems more reckless, annoying, and pointless.

When I was in junior high and early high school, I was on a soccer team that played in the highest league available. Many of the players had played together for years, bringing the team to that level of play. They thought themselves quite cool, especially given how good they were at soccer. To say they were often hostile to new players, and players they didn't consider part of the "in" crowd on the team, would be an understatement. For example, when I tried out for the team, it took the coach a while to find a specific place for me on the team. As a result, the existing players took that as a sign of weakness and added me to their list of teammates on the outs. The way some of the boys behaved towards others, including me, was really over the top at times.

Even at thirteen or fourteen, I was shocked at some of what I saw take place. I was willing to stand up for myself, so I didn't get the worst of it. However, at times, they also crossed the line with me. The core group of boys would tease and taunt people incessantly. A few of the other boys on the team were shy and weren't very self-confident. To this day, I wonder if being on that team for an extended period didn't do them some permanent harm. You could just see how they cowered when the other boys came after them. Of course, that only encouraged the bullies to keep it up. Most of the abuse was verbal, but sometimes it got physical as well. After about two years, I decided I didn't want to be in that environment and quit.

What I still find puzzling is how the parents of the boys in question, as well as the coach, allowed those boys to continue to act the way they did. The boys were often very open about their teasing and frequently did it when adults were present. Some of the adults seemed to think it was just part of growing up. I didn't agree then and don't agree now. I hope that the meanest boys changed as they grew up. If not, they probably aren't adults I'd want to associate with now either. If their attitudes didn't change, I doubt they are considered cool by many today either.

Taking Action

- Have you put too much emphasis on being viewed as cool? Have you ever done anything you regret in your efforts?

- Have you seen someone move from a status of officially cool to un-cool because he or she went too extreme with his or her behavior?

- Are you careful not to let your desire to be cool impact how you treat and behave towards others?

- Can you think of people who you respect and like because of who they are, even if they aren't officially cool? Can you think of people who are officially cool but that you really don't like much? Just be yourself and be friends with those you like and things will work out fine.

- Do you think your coworkers, friends, spouse, or children will care if you are cool? The answer should be no, so does it really matter?

Part Five

Keeping an Eye on the Future

Chapter 29
The Value of Education

As a parent, one of the most important things you can try to help your children understand is the value of an education. It is not possible to underestimate the benefits of an education in today's society. Degrees are required to get even a foot into many doors. Without a high school diploma or equivalent, it is very hard to find any job other than low-wage, low-skill jobs (and you can forget about a true career). Without a diploma, your only remote chance is to get lucky and start a business that makes it big. This, of course, will be difficult to achieve without an education related to the many aspects of running a business. It is a long shot, to say the least. Without a college degree, most high-paying jobs are out of reach. Many of the best jobs now require, or strongly prefer, advanced degrees and training that go beyond college.

When you are young, it is often un-cool to do well in school or even show that you care about it. Do not let your friends and schoolmates pull you into this mindset. Yes, there is always something more fun to do than studying and attending class, but school isn't supposed to be all fun and games. School is supposed to prepare you for the real world and give you a solid chance to succeed. While there are people who do go back and rectify bad decisions from their early years, most who blow their first shot at getting an education never make up for it. They struggle to get by for the rest of their lives and have to make do with the much more limited set of options available to them.

It is one thing to decide to take a few years to travel the world, or purposely take a job that pays very little, but you love. Choices like that can be fulfilling, and can often be associated with doing something that really makes a difference for society. Making such decisions when you know you can fall back on your education and skills is totally different from making such decisions to avoid hard work or out of a lack of other viable options.

When you are in junior high or high school and under pressure from friends to blow off schoolwork, it is hard to stay focused on the bigger picture. At that age, you can't even imagine a ten, twenty, or thirty-year time frame. This makes it even harder to do something unpleasant today in order to gain benefit sometime in the unknown future. I was there when I was young, as have all the adults in the world today. Some of us handled it better than others, just as some of your generation will. Keep a focus on your education today if you don't want to look back with regret later.

If you don't believe that education is as important as I am suggesting, think for a minute about all the resources society puts into it. We pay a lot of taxes to support schools in our local areas. We have thousands of colleges and continuing education centers around the country. Scholarships are offered by companies, foundations, the government, and schools themselves. Just think about those facts for a moment. As a society, why would we spend so much of our resources on education-related products and services unless we believe it is immensely important? Our country grew strong, in large part, through its ability to provide some of the best-educated minds to address the problems of the world and to come up with new and innovative ideas.

For you not to take your education seriously is to imply that your parents, your entire society, and the generations of people before you were all wrong, and somehow you have it figured out better. As a young person it is easy to think you know best, but is it realistic to believe that working less diligently and doing poorly in school can really lead to great things? On top of the educational impact, it puts you into a mindset and pattern that will perpetuate you doing less than you are capable of, or even failing at many things in life.

I suggest that you identify some careers that are well respected and that you can imagine yourself both doing and enjoying. Pick some that pay well and some that don't. I think you'll find that even at an entry level, most require a strong education. Teaching, medicine, science, and even being a minister in a mainstream church all require a degree or certification of some sort.

If you can maintain discipline and take your education seriously, you will have a wealth of opportunities in front of you. Even if you only go down one or two career paths in your life, you will be free to choose what interests you most. Don't limit your options just to go to one more party, or just to be a bit cooler to your unmotivated classmates and peers.

A Few Examples from My Past

I'll tell you a secret that I think made a difference in my grades in many classes in college and graduate school. With the exception of one philosophy class with a professor who literally read from the book, I NEVER missed a class except in the most dire of circumstances. It didn't matter if I had been up all night at a party. It didn't matter if I had a fever. It didn't matter if it was -15 degrees outside. I made it to class. There were several reasons for this.

First, particularly when I was in college, I thought I owed it to my parents to show up, since they were paying the bill for me to be there. It was a matter of respect. I knew I didn't like to pay for something that someone didn't use, and I didn't want my parents to do that with my college expenses.

Next, it was a way for me to force discipline on myself. I knew many others who would skip a class here or there. Then, over time, they did it more and more often. Once you start a pattern of skipping class, it is very easy to skip "just one more." Many kids did poorly in school as a result; some flunked out, and some eventually dropped out. They let go of their discipline and motivation. In general, I think setting goals and standards for yourself and then making yourself follow through is important to do. Making sure I went to class was one way I kept myself focused on discipline.

Last and most importantly, I believed that if I attended class every day, I'd hear something the professor said that ended up on the tests. This actually happened frequently. Professors will let you know what they think is important and where to put your efforts studying. Often, they'll even go so far as to say, "This will be on the test, so listen carefully." I believe professors sometimes do this specifically to reward those who come to class. Hearing the questions and discussion that classmates contribute can also provide important insights into the course material.

If you can pick up just one or two test answers every few weeks by attending class, it can make the difference between an A and a B, or a B and a C. I am convinced that I owe some of my grades to simply having shown up for class. I was able to hear points that weren't in the book, or that weren't obviously important on their own, but appeared on the test. Luckily, I proved the value of attending class to myself very early, which made it easier to continue my pattern of attending classes diligently.

The best example was when I got Mononucleosis one semester in college. It makes you feel horrible and many people can't even function. I made it to every class, even though I often had to take a nap when I got back to my room. I really struggled that semester. For a few weeks, I slept twelve to sixteen hours a day, and had trouble focusing what little energy I did have on studying and learning effectively.

In one business class, I did poorly on the second of two tests the course required when I was in the throes of the illness.

I spoke with the professor about the situation before the final exam. Since I had been in class every day, he knew I took the course seriously. He also knew I had been sick. He made a bet with me. He said something to the extent of, "Either the test you got a good grade on was a fluke, or the test you got a bad grade on was a fluke. I'll assume your final exam indicates which." I accepted his challenge.

I got a solid grade on the final and the professor gave me an A, even though my numerical average didn't quite warrant it. I attribute his kindness to the fact that he recognized that I was sincere, hardworking, and had honestly been very sick. He cut me slack. What do you think he would have done if I had missed class regularly and didn't put in an A effort? I am sure I would not have gotten that A.

Taking Action

- Are you doing everything you can to take your education seriously?

- Do you have friends who encourage you to slack off at school? How do you respond?

- Have you ever started down the slippery slope of skipping "just one class" or doing less than your best on an assignment? What made you do it, and what can you do today to reverse the trend?

- Make a list of careers you find desirable. Then, research the educational requirements tied to those careers. How many of them require a good education? (Hint: likely all!)

- Try to create a list of jobs and careers that you can validate require no education of any kind. Does the list contain enough opportunities to allow you to reach your goals in life easily?

Chapter 30
The Importance of Saving

It is very important that you start saving early and stick to it over the years. You can't count on anyone else taking care of you, especially in your old age. Instead, plan to make sure you can take care of yourself. It will seem easy to put off saving, especially when you are young. Many of your friends will probably spend everything they have each month. Don't let yourself fall into that trap.

No matter how much money you make, you can put some away. Decide on an amount and put it away every month. Consider it a bill that you have to pay, just like taxes and electricity. You'll quickly learn to live without the amount you save. Also, when you get a raise, consider putting a good portion, if not all, of the raise toward your savings. You are already used to living without the raise, so just continue that way. Invest your savings wisely and don't just leave it in a checking or savings account for the long term. How to invest is outside the scope of this chapter, but there is plenty of information available on the topic.

Once you have established the pattern of having money going to savings each month, it will be very easy to continue it except in extreme circumstances. It is amazing how many people will say they can't afford to save, yet they'll have a new phone, new clothes, and a nice car. It isn't that they can't afford to save, but that they don't choose to save and prioritize saving over living for the moment.

Don't fail to recognize that there is a huge difference between income and wealth. Many people with very high incomes have no wealth because they spend everything they earn, no matter how much they are earning. They are living just a few paychecks from a total financial meltdown just as much as the person earning only minimum wage. The high earners just live more comfortably as they sit on a monetary cliff. To have real security, you'll need to save and grow wealth, not just have a high income. Simply living a little below your means throughout life will allow you to live comfortably after you retire.

I focused on saving from the time I was still in school. In graduate school, I managed to save about $50/month from my $1,000 per month stipend. Full-time tuition was only about $600 per semester at the time. My rent was $300 per month, I rode a bike to class, and I worked in the summer to make some extra cash. Most people come out of graduate school with a lot of debt. I came out of graduate school with a few thousand dollars in savings.

Granted, I was very lucky that the school I attended was far less expensive than many and the area had a very low cost of living. However, I had an old tabletop placed over milk crates for my living room table, a cot for my couch, a beanbag chair, and a mattress directly on the floor. I focused on keeping my expenses down. I knew plenty of people in my class who accumulated a lot more debt by living above their means in much nicer apartments with much nicer furnishings.

From my first paycheck when I started my career, I automatically had money put into savings. Each year, as I received raises, I always increased the amount I saved. As a result, my accounts really built up over time. I set it up so that my brokerage account would deduct money from my checking account each month at the same time my rent was due. My checking account considered it a required bill. When I needed to dip into my savings for a short-term issue, I did so. However, having to go to the separate account made it impossible for me to pretend that I wasn't hitting my savings. I considered it a loan when I dipped into my savings, and I always had a plan to pay the money back.

Saving on a regular basis will take discipline and sacrifice, but it will be worth the effort to know you'll be able to take care of your family and yourself. I know many people who didn't think about saving until they were much older. At that point, the burden is much higher. Not only do you have to make up for the savings you missed previously, but you have to make up for all the missed growth in the funds that would have accrued over time as well. Those who wait too long simply can't catch up and have a secure retirement, let alone pass on money to their heirs.

Unless something catastrophic occurs, nobody will have to worry about my wife or me when we get old. That's how we want it. Everyone has enough of their own worries without worrying about us. We also hope to pass on some inheritance. We will be able to do these things only because of our diligence and discipline over the years. Saving just wasn't an option. It was part of our duty to ourselves and our family.

A Few Examples from My Past

I was sold on the idea of saving after my first look at a compound interest chart. It showed how money saved at a 15 percent annual return would grow. Every five years or so, the money doubles. In five years, $1 becomes $2. In ten years, it is $4. In fifteen years, it is $8. Look at a compound interest graph and you'll see how the money explodes not in a linear fashion, but in an exponential fashion. In other words, the money grows faster and faster as time passes.

While 15 percent returns seem a thing of the past as I write this, the same general pattern emerges with any interest rate. It is just a faster or slower pace of exponential growth based on the average rate of return. One simple guideline is the *Rule of 72*. Divide your rate of return into seventy-two and that is approximately how many years it will take your money to double. So, a 15 percent average return will take about five years to double your money ($72 \div 15 = 4.8$) and a 5 percent return will take fifteen years to double your money ($72 \div 5 = 14.4$).

The key is to have enough time to get into the zone of huge gains that starts after the first few doublings. That's why starting young like I did is so important. It gives you time to double your investments more times than would be achieved if you start later.

Another big lesson for me was seeing some statistics on saving in an Individual Retirement Account (IRA). The facts that I have never forgotten were part of an example in an article I read. It goes like this: Person 1 saves $2,000 per year from age twenty-five to age thirty-five and then never saves another penny. Person 2 saves $2,000 per year starting at age thirty-five and does it every year after that until death. They both earn 10 percent returns on average. Believe it or not, Person 1 will have more money than Person 2 no matter how old they both live to be. In fact, Person 1 can have many times more money than Person 2 depending on the average return. The same pattern emerges with any realistic rate of return.

The reason for that outcome comes down to the time value of money and compound interest. Person 1 was able to start with a decade of money that was already into the growth cycle. The later contributions from person 2 just can't catch up unless the average rate of return is extremely low. Start saving early and it pays.

I have another tip for you that can help you keep your spending priorities straight. I have always tracked all of my income and expenditures with a package called Quicken. It forces me to think about what I am spending and led to a little habit that some people think is crazy. When debating a large purchase, I will ask, "Would I rather have this thing for $XX now or would I rather have five to ten times $XX in twenty years by saving the money instead of spending it today?" I often choose to save when faced with the facts in that way. There were many times that I could have easily afforded something, but I didn't need the item and I found that the satisfaction of knowing I didn't spend frivolously was greater than the satisfaction of yet another unneeded toy. Sometimes, of course, I did make a big purchase. After applying the preceding test, I knew I was comfortable with the purchase.

Let's return to my comment about tracking all my income and expenses with Quicken. Keeping careful tabs on what you're earning and spending is critical no matter how much you decide to save. By keeping on top of exactly where you stand financially, it will be hard to make a mistake like overdrawing your account or committing to too many ongoing expenses. I believe the root issue with many who don't save isn't as much that they don't want to save, but that they don't watch their money carefully enough to ensure they can stick to the discipline of saving. If you manage your money by simply making sure there is enough cash in the account to cover the check you're about to write, you'll never be on top of your finances. Take your finances very seriously even when you first start out in life with little money to worry about. You should always know exactly where your finances stand.

Taking Action

- Have you thought about how you'll pay your bills, and have some money left over to enjoy yourself in retirement? If not, start today.

- Do you save now? If not, will you commit to starting this month?

- Have you learned some basic home finance skills? If not, consider a class or begin to do your own research.

- Have you ever seen the impact of compound interest? If not, experiment with an online compound interest tool. What you see should motivate you to save.

- If you aren't thinking of how you'll finance your retirement, who else do you expect is going to do it? What's stopping you from taking ownership of your future?

Chapter 31
You Will Compete
Against the Whole World

Back when I first started working in the early 1990's, people in the United States were almost exclusively competing amongst themselves in most careers. This was especially true in professional fields. We didn't have the Internet, or cell phones, or email. Long distance calls were very, very expensive within the US and even worse if you called internationally.

As a result, we had to go to an office every day to get work done. It just wasn't possible to work from home or anywhere else. You had to be there in person. What this meant is that you didn't have to compete with people from other parts of the world. If they weren't living in the US, they couldn't plausibly do your job.

However, things changed rapidly and by the time I became a dad, most Americans were competing with non-Americans for work. Between virtually free phone calls, email, file sharing, and other technologies, it really didn't matter where a worker was located. I frequently worked from home when my children were little. The people I worked with wouldn't have known the difference if I had been halfway around the world instead of downstairs. So, while it was good for me, it was also a new risk. If I could do much of my work from home, somebody else somewhere else could do it, too. Worse for me, they might be willing to do it for much less money.

You can expect this trend will only continue. You will be competing for jobs against a global workforce. That's billions of people. You will need to be prepared and will need to work hard to earn your spot. Many Americans don't realize this and have let their skills get outdated or, worse, gotten lazy. In sports, if a team doesn't show up ready to win, they will usually lose. Winning is as dependant on a mindset as it is a skill set. You not only need to build up your skills, you'll need to show up to win every day.

Programming computers was a very lucrative field when I started my career. That changed rapidly. I recall when programming jobs started to move to other countries. People around the world were willing to work for a fraction of what Americans were being paid. Not only that, but technology had advanced to where a programmer in another country could connect to a company network and write code just as well as someone in a cube or working from home here in the United States.

I wasn't too worried about the programmers, since that wasn't what I did. However, the trend did concern me. Who was to say what jobs would be next? Eventually, many companies began to outsource partially what I do for a living. I was lucky that I was senior enough when this started happening that I held positions that couldn't really be outsourced. I had too much client interaction and needed to be local in the US. However, the people down the chain from me today will have more of a struggle than I did to get to where I am today.

You have to expect that you'll be competing with people from all over the world from day one. Be prepared. Don't underestimate how eager people in other countries are to increase their living standard. If you were born and raised in America, you have pretty much been spoiled all your life. You may not feel spoiled compared to some of your friends, but compared to those in many other countries, we're all spoiled. Many people in the world struggle to survive. For them, the job they take with an American company isn't just something to pay the bills. It is literally a shot out of poverty and a chance to change everything for themselves and their families. As a result, they will be willing to work harder than you can imagine, even as they make much less money than you. This means you're going to have to find a way to work hard, differentiate yourself, and make a company need you personally. You can't strive to be just another face in the crowd doing a good job and expect to succeed.

This theme ties back to some of the others in this book. Take your education seriously and work hard. If you slack off and aren't at the top of your game, you'll be watching from the sideline as someone from elsewhere beats you to the jobs you want and need. You'll have many friends who aren't inclined to work very hard. When you're ahead of them, you may feel like you can take it easy and still keep a comfortable lead. The problem is that the serious competition isn't your friends. Soon you'll be competing with people you've never met, from all over the world. Do the best you can do and don't just aim to beat whoever you're up against on any given day. Eventually you'll be up against others who are even better and you need to be prepared. It will be a completely different level of competition. Many athletes can't transition from college sports to professional sports. Similarly, many students who did great compared to their peers in school may find themselves not able to keep up when they try to play at the next level in their career.

If things keep going the way they are as I write this, I worry about what opportunities will be available to young Americans in the future. At the same time, I believe that very smart people who have needed skills and are willing to work hard will always have a place in America and the world as a whole. You increase your odds of success by ensuring your skills are solidly built and that you are someone that nobody doubts will work hard and get the job done right.

A Few Examples from My Past

As I mentioned previously, when my children were small I worked from home if I wasn't travelling. I started to do that in 2000. The positive side was that I didn't need to drive to an office to do my job and was able to have more time with my kids. The negative side is that for much of what I was doing, the fact that I wasn't in an office put me on a more equal footing with people in developing countries.

Jobs in my field—analytics—started being shipped outside the United States in the late 2000's. It was very disconcerting for me. I was lucky enough to be advanced enough in my career so that people needed me to be present in person on a regular basis. The catch is that I learned the skills that got me to that point by doing analysis in my early years. As the jobs I did early in my career move to other countries, there will be fewer opportunities for the next generation to gain the same basic skills I learned. Find a career that appears to have a reasonable chance of still letting you earn a living while residing in the US.

One scenario I've seen played out in sports and academics is something that you need to be aware of. When I grew up playing soccer, it wasn't nearly as popular and widespread as it is today. Soccer was quite big in certain parts of the country, like the Washington, DC area but in large parts of the country people barely played it. I recall times my team would play a powerhouse team from another part of Virginia or somewhere else in the country. These teams hardly ever lost and were used to winning all the time. We easily crushed them.

How did we do that? It was simple. We were playing on another level. The teams we were playing from elsewhere hadn't been exposed to our level of competition and weren't ready for us, even though they may have thought they were. It is a hard lesson the first time this happens. There are stories like that in virtually every sport and it still happens today. There are also stories of the top students from very small towns struggling or failing at a major university. It isn't that they aren't smart; they just didn't receive the quality of teaching and peer competition they needed to develop. They crushed the competition at their school, but were still unprepared for a big league university.

I was on the losing end of this concept once. In graduate school, I entered the university racquetball tournament. Well over 100 people had entered. As I advanced in the tournament I started to think I had really improved my skills. In the quarter-finals and semi-finals, I beat players I couldn't believe I beat. They had better skills, but I was faster and had a better reach. I won and went into the final thinking I was playing at a top level.

The final started out 7–7 in the first game and I was feeling good about my chances and my performance. Then the guy I was playing against realized that I actually could play and he couldn't just take it easy and beat me like he had likely done in every other match. He started to play his best and he absolutely crushed me. The first game ended something like 15–9 and the second was something like 15–4. He dominated me and I couldn't hang with him at all. He was on a totally different level than I was. I didn't even know that level existed until I experienced it by playing him. It was quite humbling, but also a very good lesson in not getting too comfortable with my abilities.

Remember, whenever you think you can coast a little since you're winning among your current peers, there may be others out there playing with a different set of people on a much higher level. When you find those others, try to play with them. If you're going to ensure you can compete on your highest level, seek out the strongest competition that you can handle to maximize your chances in the world. Never assume that just because you're at the top of your peers there isn't still plenty of room for improvement and that others elsewhere might just crush you.

Taking Action

- Have you ever had an experience where you thought you were good at something and then ran into someone else much better who showed you how much you had to learn?

- Do you make a point to remind yourself regularly that you need to be ready to compete with the best in the world, not just the best in your current peer group?

- Make a list of careers that interest you. Then, identify those that are easy to do from anywhere in the world and those that really need someone locally. The latter may be a better choice.

- Research the typical standard of living for people in other countries. It will help you realize why Americans have it pretty good and why those in other countries are thrilled with what we view as a low paycheck.

- If you haven't already, commit to seeking out people currently better than you at something and compete with them to build your skills and help you reach your potential.

Chapter 32
Assume What You Do
Will Become Public Knowledge

Kids today are growing up in a very different world than I did. I'm sure that by the time you read this, things will have changed so much that some of what I've written will already seem dated, but the main theme—assume that anything you say or do might become public knowledge—will still hold true. So, you must be very careful.

When I grew up, unless somebody took a picture (which was expensive and was not typically done on a whim) or wrote something down by hand, there was really no record of anything you did. Email didn't even exist. In cases when something actually was recorded, there would be one copy of what someone wrote or one printed picture to worry about. It was very, very rare that anything embarrassing that you did was known to anyone that wasn't there. Over time, any traces would be gone.

Today, we have Twitter, Facebook, digital cameras, and cameras and voice recorders built into mobile phones. Not only can anything you say or do be recorded, but it can be disseminated easily and immediately. To make things worse, digital records on the web can't ever really be erased. Once something is out there, it is out there. I frequently read things today about people who have been greatly embarrassed and hurt based on something they did a long time ago because it was posted somewhere and somebody managed to find and expose it.

The reason you have to be careful is that when you're young, you tend to do stupid things. To make matters worse, you won't be thinking ahead to how the acts might impact you later. I did some stupid things when I was younger. Luckily, there is no record of them, but if there was, it would be quite embarrassing now.

People lose jobs due to pictures or comments they've posted on the Internet. Worse, someone else can post pictures of you or say things about you that hurt you later. You have no control over what others post other than not letting them have the harmful picture or comment in the first place. The only way to be totally safe is to really try to think about what you are doing and be very careful. It is unfortunate that you can't be as carefree as I was when I was younger, but times have changed.

One way to train yourself is to think about how you'd feel if your mom and dad found out exactly what you are about to say or do. If the thought makes you cringe, you better think twice. It is entirely possible they will find out. There is an entire chapter dedicated to this concept earlier in the book (See Chapter 11: Think About How Your Actions Would Look to Your Parents). I have not yet had something from the Internet influence a hiring or firing decision I have made, but I imagine it will happen eventually. I'd hate for something you do today to cost you a job opportunity much later in life. Worse, I'd hate for something from your past to badly embarrass you in front of your friends and family or cause pain to them in the distant future.

You can often read in the news about a young man or woman who allowed photos to be taken when they either were undressed or participating in "private activities." Next thing the person knows, the photos are going viral all over the Internet and all around their school. This can be quite embarrassing and can devastate a young person's life. Worse, if the subject of the photo is under 18 years of age, anyone in possession of the photo or forwarding it on can be prosecuted for child pornography!

There aren't many things worse than being convicted of child pornography and having to register as a sex offender for the rest of your life. It doesn't seem fair that teens taking pictures of themselves and their friends would count the same as true child pornography, but that is how the laws are today. What seems like a harmless snapshot for a boyfriend or girlfriend can actually land you in jail and ruin your life. You have to be careful.

A tangential topic to this is tattoos and other permanent body modifications. Please think long and hard before you get any. Tattoos didn't become widely popular until I was in my thirties. You must remember that tattoos and many other body modifications are permanent. By the time you read this, you'll probably have the pleasure of seeing your friends' moms and dads with tattoos that don't necessarily seem to make sense for their age and place in life. Perhaps the tattoos made sense when they were younger, but today they might not. Better yet, just wait a few more years for the grandmas and grandpas to show up at the beach with their tattoos or big ear hoops. It doesn't sound as appealing as it does to see young people with the same, does it?

If you get a tattoo or permanent body modification, be ready to have it for life. You also have to be aware that a tattoo absolutely can cost you a job. Many people and companies will not hire anyone with a visible tattoo. A tattoo that can't be covered with typical business attire just won't cut it in the professional world I work in, nor would a huge hole in an earlobe. Something that seems like a fun, rebellious act can eliminate you from many good jobs. Maybe you won't want a corporate job, but then again, maybe you will. Why risk eliminating those possibilities? If you must get a tattoo or body modification, get one somewhere that can be kept hidden in situations where it needs to be.

Call me an old fuddy-duddy if you want, but you may run into plenty of hiring managers in the years to come who will be fuddy-duddies just like me. Color your hair purple all you want, or get a Mohawk. Those can be reversed. Don't do anything permanent without serious consideration first.

A Few Examples from My Past

I did some stupid things when I was young. I really don't want to share the details about the times I was lucky that nobody had a phone with a camera or a Twitter account handy to broadcast my stupidity. If it isn't public now, I won't make it so!

However, I am truly lucky that some of my less proud moments aren't captured in a photo or in a blog for the entire world to see. It would be embarrassing and harmful. Now, I always think more carefully before I act than I used to. Part of it is due to my work, partly due to age, and partly due to the new realities. I wish I didn't have to think twice, but it is better to be safe than sorry. At times you'll feel like you're thinking too much, missing too much fun, or being too paranoid. However, all it takes is getting burnt badly once and you won't complain again about being careful. I hope you don't learn your lessons in too harsh a way. And, I hope your parents aren't the ones who see a record of it!

I have a funny but true story. A man I worked with had a son who was twenty. The two were also friends on Facebook. One night my coworker was on a business trip and he got a Facebook update. It was a picture of his son at a party holding a beer. Then, he noticed that his son was sitting in his house. Last, he noticed the time stamp on the photo was just a few minutes earlier. His son was having a secret party while Dad was out of town! He called his son and shut the party down. The son was totally busted. In this case, the "gotcha" was somewhat harmless, but it illustrates why you have to be careful. Someone else posted a picture of the party with the man's son tagged and it gave away their sneaky secret party. Once the picture was posted, my co-worker was able to see it since his son's name was tagged to it.

When I was in high school, boys wearing earrings was a new trend and it was considered somewhat rebellious. An earring on one side represented a straight, but rebellious boy, while an earring on the other side showed that you were gay. I don't recall which side was which and I don't think that rule has applied for many years now.

I remember a trip to Atlantic City, New Jersey for a soccer tournament when I was sixteen or seventeen. Several of the boys on the team got their ears pierced at a shop on the boardwalk. I can still see the coach's sons being berated by their grandfather in the middle of the boardwalk for their earrings. He was so unhappy and angry that he couldn't control himself. Several other parents also were quite displeased.

As a joke, my friend and I went and bought some earrings that had a number of small pieces attached. We removed the pieces and were able to get one of the pieces to clip onto our ear in a way that made it look like it was a real piercing. I remember walking down on the beach and saying hello to my parents to see their reaction. Given all the controversy with the other boys, their eyes quickly went to my ear. Instead of saying anything, my dad just got up and walked away. I hadn't seen him that upset in a while. After a few minutes, I let my mom in on the joke. She was relieved, but told me that I needed to let my dad know quickly because she hadn't seen such a strong reaction from him in a while and he was not getting the joke at all. He was relieved when I showed him the trick I had done.

Occasionally I would wear that fake earring for fun, but since I didn't have a permanent piercing, it left no mark. I don't have a hole or scar on my ear today. While the reactions to the earrings that I experienced seem extreme today, it was very much standard back then. There are temporary tattoos and many other ways to experiment and express yourself without getting something permanent. Consider those options first.

Taking Action

- Do you know anyone who has been embarrassed because something they thought was done in private went public? Has it happened to you?

- Do you make yourself stop and think about how what you are doing, or thinking of doing, would reflect on you if it became public?

- Are you courteous to others by being prudent about what you post, related to them, without their permission? If you embarrass others, intentionally or not, they may get you back when given the chance.

- Have you and your friends discussed the boundaries of what you agree is okay to post to the Internet, or otherwise capture, and what is not?

- If you ever find yourself considering a permanent body modification, think long and hard. Decide if you think the modification will still look cool when you are a parent or grandparent. Also consider how people in the workplace might react. If you aren't certain you'll have no regrets, don't do it.

Chapter 33
Treat Everyone Well and It Will Pay Off

Treating people well is the right thing to do. It's that simple. You shouldn't treat anyone poorly unless you want to be treated poorly right back. However, there is another reason that you should treat people well: it goes beyond common manners and decency. While it is a bit self-serving, it is also quite motivational. The fact is that when you treat people well, they will in turn treat you well. You'll be amazed at how simply being nice and respectful can help you get ahead.

Some people are arrogant, impatient, or mean. This can lead them to treat others poorly. Perhaps the worst cases are when someone who is powerful or famous treats badly those less powerful or famous. This often happens because one person feels they are "better" than the other person. You can often see this attitude in action in the way people treat others who are in roles—waitress, cashier, administrative assistant—which are considered "below" many other roles. I find it most obnoxious when someone acts out of an assumption that another person is subservient to them and isn't worthy of respect. Please don't ever be that way because it makes you look like a jerk. Worse, if you actually start to believe that you are above others on a regular basis, you've lost your grounding and need to have an attitude adjustment.

Growing up, I often heard an old rule about always treating the assistant to an executive well. When I was in school, this didn't make sense to me. After all, why does the administrative assistant matter? It is not that I ever planned to treat assistants badly. Rather, I just didn't understand why they would be singled out for good treatment, given their low position on the organizational chart. It seemed like focus should be on the executive.

Once I got into the working world, I realized why this rule exists. You would be amazed at the power administrative assistants have to help or hurt you in obtaining access to their bosses. If they like you, they'll find a way to get you a meeting or to pass a message from you. If they don't like you, you may hear that the boss is too busy to meet, or the assistant's policy is not to pass on unsolicited messages. There is no way for you to verify if they are telling the truth and you're at their mercy if they respond this way.

The point is that the "lowly" assistant is probably a very nice, hardworking person who deserves your respect unless they do something to lose it. It astonishes me how arrogantly and poorly many people treat the administrative assistants that I have worked with. People who are very nice overall will turn into jerks when dealing with people they consider to be far down the chain from them. It is rude and uncalled for.

Also make sure to keep your frustrations or emotions in check when dealing with service personnel. This might include a server at a restaurant, a mechanic, a flight attendant, a cashier, or a customer service agent, among others. These people make their living interacting with others. In many cases, they specifically have to deal with people when something has gone wrong. You may be mad, or frustrated, or upset . . . and it may be for good reason. However, that doesn't mean you have to take it out on the person who has the unenviable task of helping you resolve your issue. Just remember that until someone proves otherwise, you should assume that he or she is a good, hardworking person who will try to resolve your problem the best way he or she can. Your problem usually isn't the fault of the person you're dealing with; they are simply the one assigned to help you fix it.

By being nice, you not only do the right thing, but you provide relief to people who may be tired of being treated poorly. They will be happy with how you're handling the situation and you'll get their best effort. Never forget that there are many options available for how someone can help you. You will not know all the options at his or her disposal, but he or she certainly will. Which options you are offered can depend greatly on how you're behaving.

As you go through life always make an effort to treat people nicely, no matter how stressful of a situation you are in. Also be sure to be respectful of others regardless of their official position in the hierarchy of life. On top of being the right thing to do, it will also pay dividends for you. Everyone is happy to help someone they think treats them in a genuinely respectful manner.

A Few Examples from My Past

Some of the nicest people I have ever known were far from the most prominent people I have known. Over the years, some of the administrative assistants and handymen I met turned out to be truly amazing people. I counted myself lucky to have gotten to know them and to appreciate the way in which they did their jobs and lived their lives. Stories abound of immigrants from other parts of the world that came to the United States with a PhD, but didn't speak our language. As a result, they worked as a janitor or in some other "lowly" role so that their children could have the benefit of growing up in this country. Always give people a chance, regardless of their position in life. You will be impressed with many of those you meet once you get to know them. Many of your peers will miss out since they won't be able to get past their snobbery.

I travelled heavily for a number of years when my children were young. As a result, I had my fair share of travel disasters with delayed or cancelled flights, messed up hotel reservations, or lost car reservations. People can be at their worst in such situations. I am always amazed by how the gate agents and flight attendants are able to keep their composure and stay professional when someone is getting very nasty with them. I don't think I could handle such a position very well and I respect those who can. What they do sometimes, however, is keep smiling while they purposely do less than they could to help the person who is behaving badly. It is a passive-aggressive, stealth attack that the rude person doesn't even realize has hit them.

Once I was in line behind someone yelling at a gate agent about the need to get on another flight fast after our flight was cancelled. The man got on the first flight the next morning and walked away thinking that he had won. When I got to the counter, I made a comment about what a jerk the last guy had been and commended the agent on how she handled him. When we got to talking about how to rebook me, she suddenly "found" another flight option a few hours later, as opposed to the next day. She smiled as she explained that she must have missed that one while helping the prior gentleman. Had he been nice, he would have gotten on my flight.

I have also experienced numerous occasions when a restaurant was packed and understaffed. It is easy to tell if a waiter or waitress is bad at the job or if there are simply too many tables to handle. If the latter, there isn't much your server can do but try their best. Imagine how frustrating it is for them to know they aren't serving their customers well, their customers are very unhappy, and their tips are going to suffer even as they work extra hard.

Getting mad at the servers won't do anything except make their day worse. Have a heated exchange with the manager who didn't schedule enough people if you must, but not the servers. On more than one occasion when I was kind to a struggling server throughout a meal, he or she would thank me. This might include only a verbal thank you, but it also often involved a dessert arriving on the house, or a round of drinks being removed from the bill. I am sure that if I had been yelling at the servers I would not have received such treatment. Those gestures of gratitude helped me feel better about the experience, save a little money as compensation for the bad service, and encouraged me to tip the server very well with a clean conscience. The server earned his or her tip and the restaurant took the hit for not being appropriately staffed.

Of course, there have been times that I have let my frustration get the best of me and I have taken it out on someone who really wasn't responsible. I must admit there have been times that I've turned into the very person I have been disparaging throughout this chapter. Those who witnessed my behavior probably assumed that's how I act all the time. I am always quite embarrassed after such an incident. In fact, it embarrasses me that I have been guilty of such behavior more than once. Over time, I have become much, much better at stopping it from happening by making myself step back and calm down.

Your goal should be to minimize how many incidents of behaving badly it takes you to gain the same control over yourself. Treat everyone with respect, regardless of their position. The good vibes that you project will come back to you in a big way.

Taking Action

- Are you careful not to look down on others regardless of what their status is in life?

- Have you ever been looked down upon or treated badly by someone else? How did it make you feel? Would you want to make others feel that way?

- Do you recognize who is actually at fault, as opposed to who is trying to help you deal with a difficult situation? The two are often not the same and your actions should reflect that.

- Make two lists. On one, list ways that you think being disrespectful and condescending to others will help you get ahead in life. On the other, list ways that being respectful of others will do the same. Which list is longer?

- Can you think of times in your past when you were embarrassed by what you thought of others or how you treated them? What can you do differently next time?

Chapter 34
Having Children

One of the biggest decisions you'll face in life is whether or not (and when) to have children. Just a generation or two ago, it was assumed that people would get married very young and immediately start having children. If someone had fertility issues, of course, they might not succeed, but very few people chose not to have kids if they were able to.

These days, it is more common for people to choose not to have children. Everyone can make their own choices, but I strongly believe that becoming a parent is something that everyone should consider if physically and mentally fit to do so. Many who choose not to have kids do so in order to focus on their careers. Some make the choice because they think it would be too disruptive to their lifestyle. Some just think it would be too much work.

Speaking from experience, kids do pose challenges to a career path, they do disrupt your lifestyle, and they do take a lot of work. However, I don't think anyone I know would trade in the experience. Did I miss going out with my friends on a

Friday night? Sure, but honestly, when my kids were babies I truly preferred to stay home and play with them and let them fall asleep on me. My childless friends, especially those who weren't even married, couldn't imagine that my priorities could be so changed. In fact, when I was single and childless, I couldn't imagine myself thinking that way either. Once you have a baby, however, the changes are welcome and happy.

Children can bring a level of happiness and fulfillment to your life that is hard to understand without going through it. You'll never feel like you're ready to have kids, even when you are expecting one. If you wait around until everything seems perfect before having a baby, you'll probably miss your chance. At some point, you just have to jump into parenthood and trust that you're more ready than you think. Once the first baby comes, the vast majority of people figure parenting out very quickly. Changing your lifestyle or passing on a great career move that would take too much time from your familial duties doesn't seem so bad when you're looking at a baby or young child.

I very consciously made some choices that were not the best for my career and earning power in order to try to be a good dad. It really didn't bother me at all, which surprised me since I am so competitive. I think the reason is that my competitiveness led me to want to be very good at the "dad game," too. I decided that I'd rather win the dad game than the work game if it came down to a choice. It was easy to make the decisions required to do so.

Unless you have issues that prevent you from having children, please consider making the choice to have some once you are older and married. It is an innate, natural part of human life and of life in the world in general. I think people are hardwired to desire and enjoy being parents. Just think of the opportunity it affords you to help another generation make their way in the world, using the guidance that you can provide from your experience. If I hadn't had kids, I never would have thought about many of the issues in this book and I certainly never would have written it. Writing this has really helped me focus on the lessons in the book as well. What might you miss out on if you don't have kids?

I cannot stress enough that when I discuss having children, I am assuming a few critical factors. First, you are old enough to bear the responsibility. Second, you married and committed to raising children with a spouse. Third, you are prepared to change your lifestyle to meet the requirements of being a parent. These three criteria are critical.

When you look at poverty trends, two of the biggest factors associated with poverty are having children when you are young, and being a single parent. Having a baby as a single teen is one of the worst combinations. Being a parent is hard enough when you have a spouse to help and you're mature enough to handle it. Being a parent by yourself when you are very young makes it even harder. To have children voluntarily as a single person brings along many additional challenges. I strongly suggest you don't go that route.

The willingness to change your lifestyle is also critical. Many children struggle in school and life because their parents don't give them the attention and priority that they deserve. Children aren't meant to figure out how to live on their own. If parents are not around to teach and discipline their children, it puts the children at great risk for developing bad habits and getting into trouble. Children are not collectibles. You can't take them out when you are in the mood and put them away when you are not. It is a full-time job for at least 18 years. You aren't being fair to your children if you don't enter into parenthood with this expectation and a commitment to take parenting seriously.

A Few Examples from My Past

There are people I know who badly wanted to have children, but were unable. I feel horrible for them and can sympathize with how they feel. My wife and I had immense trouble having children ourselves. In fact, for some time it seemed a very real possibility that we wouldn't succeed. We had a few very stressful years as we tried all sorts of treatments to have a baby. We were pretty close to giving up when it finally worked. Had we not succeeded, our only options would have been to adopt or to forego having children altogether. I know more than one person who has gone the adoption route, which has its own long and stressful process. However, everyone I know who went through it thinks it was worth it. We never had to decide whether or not we'd go the adoption route because our luck changed and we succeeded in having our children.

I can't tell you how happy I am that we had our children. They have been an amazing addition to both my life and my wife's. It has been a wonderful experience getting to raise them and see them grow, though they both posed challenges at times. In fact, the name of this book comes from their favorite tantrum scream, "I need to tell you something!" I wish the line hadn't been used as much as it was, but kids have tantrums and it is part of growing up. Putting up with some less-than-stellar behavior from them at times is a small price to pay for all the good times they brought us. I hope that you'll get to experience it for yourselves one day. I even look forward to watching my grandchildren have a tantrum and being able to tell my kids, "I know exactly where they got that from!"

I have also known some people who seemed to have more of a selfish attitude about children. It wasn't that they were unable to have children; they didn't want their life disrupted. They didn't want to worry about getting home instead of doing whatever it took to climb the corporate ladder. They had workout schedules, hobbies, and other activities that they didn't want to have to alter. That's their choice to make. However, I have always wondered if they might not regret that decision later in life. As I stated previously, I think humans are hardwired to be parents. Avoiding that calling voluntarily must cause an internal conflict somewhere. As these people age, end their career, and wind down their lives, I wonder what it will be like. Who will check on them? Who will help them when they need it? Family is the best security net, and often the only one, that people have. Without a family to fall back on, they may come to regret their decision not to have children.

Taking Action

- Do you expect to have children one day? Why or why not?

- Have you considered the sacrifices that your parents make for you recently? There are probably more than you give them credit for.

- Do you want to give your children the best chance to succeed in the world? If so, wait until you are older, married, and ready to commit to being a parent.

- Do you know anyone being raised in a single parent household? Are there some extra challenges they face as a result?

- When is the last time you thanked your parents for all they have done for you? Consider thanking them today.

Chapter 35
Exercising Your Right to Vote

One of the primary ways you get to guide the future is by taking advantage of your right to vote. In the United States, we are lucky that we are able to vote directly on many important issues and to elect people who will guide the decisions being made. Not all countries have similar rights. In many countries, freedom is extremely limited and oppression is high. There were brave people who gave their lives so that we can live the way we do in this country and have the opportunity to vote. Do not squander that opportunity.

It can seem like your vote doesn't count. After all, it is just one of millions of votes. However, if everyone stayed home under the assumption their vote didn't count, nothing would get done. I believe that you can't complain about anything that happens because of an election if you didn't vote. If you vote and your candidate loses or your ballot question fails to pass, then complain all you want. Just make sure that you take advantage of the opportunity to have your say.

When preparing to vote, please take the time to be informed on the candidates and issues. There is much misinformation spread by the media and even the candidates themselves. Carefully examine the facts and make up your own mind. I believe that many problems our country faces are a result of the fact that too many voters show up and vote without really understanding what they are voting for and against. They think they are voting for something they support, but in fact are voting for something they wouldn't support if they understood the facts in detail. Just listening to sound bites and talking points can lead you down the wrong path.

You will also need to determine what your overall political philosophy is. You will realize, as you get older, what direction your parents lean, but that shouldn't influence you too much. Make your own decisions on key issues. Do you want limited government? Or do you want bigger government? Do you want the government staying out of your life to the maximum extent possible? Or do you want the government heavily involved in your life? Do you believe that people should help themselves and that you should help others through private means when necessary? Or do you believe that government should be the primary source of help? Do you want our society to enforce some strong moral standards on everyone? Or do you believe that each individual should choose what's right for them? These are all decisions you will need to make. Then you will have the opportunity to choose candidates for office who share your view. I hope you'll vote every chance you get so that the country will have a brighter future as you help define its future direction with your vote.

If we continue down the path we are going as I write this, the country will be in trouble. Among other things, I believe that unless we make some changes, we will be bankrupt before those currently in school are my age. While the majority of the country would agree we're heading down the wrong path, the solutions people support can be strikingly different and even completely opposite. Decide where you stand through your own research and soul searching. You shouldn't follow your parents voting patterns and outlook simply because it is what you saw them do. Rather, I hope that you'll conclude on your own which way you want to go.

A Few Examples from My Past

I really tried to shy away from espousing specific political views in this book and think I succeeded. Even in this chapter I tried to avoid guiding you to one view or another, but rather to lay out some examples of the choices you'll have to make as you decide where you fall. The primary way people classify politics is the liberal (left wing) approach on one side and the conservative (right wing) approach on the other. There are some substantial differences in viewpoints and desired actions as you move along the spectrum from the far left to the far right. People can fall anywhere in the spectrum. The implementation of policies based on the political leanings of those elected can drastically change how society looks and how we live over time. Make sure you understand where politicians fall on the spectrum and how they match your views so that you can vote correctly.

I have come to believe that, in a perfect world, our political choices would be much easier. If life was fair, everyone was equally motivated and honest, and everyone got along, most policies would probably work well and we wouldn't need nearly as many of them. However, life isn't fair, everyone isn't equally motivated and honest, and everyone does not get along. There are unfortunate realities that we have to deal with and take into account. Depending on where you are on the political spectrum, you'll desire very different plans to deal with those realities.

When I push for a certain policy, it is because I think it is the best way to deal with the realities we must face. Often, in my opinion, people pushing for policies don't deal with realities. They aim for what's ideal instead of what's realistic, they decide based on what someone else told them, or they decide based on what is best for them in the short term instead of looking at what is best for the country in the long term. Ideally, people would use government assistance as a short-term stopgap when they hit hard times. In reality, many people get addicted to it and are never motivated to get off of the assistance. What should we do about that and should we even care? How you vote can decide what actually happens.

It is always easy to point to some specific child, elderly person, or poor person who will be helped by any proposed policy. You can always find someone who will be hurt by any proposed policy, too. Anything that impacts the collection of money through taxes and how it is distributed will lead to some winners and losers. People supporting a particular policy may ask you why you couldn't support their policy, since it will help some kids. They'll ask how you could be so heartless as to consider how that policy would be paid for. It is the "right thing to do," after all, and we'll figure it out. How can you put a price on helping kids? Unfortunately, the bills will eventually come due and if you can't afford them, you're in trouble. Carefully think through the implications of a policy, as well as how it will be funded. Otherwise you risk not only failing to help those you intended, but possibly causing them harm over time if a policy falls apart.

How could you be against helping kids in every way possible? It sounds very appealing. You want to help kids, so why not support whatever policy is being suggested? The reason is that you have to ask harder questions. Is this an efficient way to help kids, or are there other ways to help even more kids? Is the program actually affordable? What other opportunities will be bypassed and not pursued due to lack of funding because of funds being diverted to the proposed program? Will the program actually achieve the goals it laid out?

There is an old phrase: "The road to hell is paved with good intentions." As you reach voting age, assess the issues with facts. Much damage can be done by people who mean well, but are misguided and don't think through the complexities that a seemingly simple program or policy can produce. Just because something sounds good doesn't mean it will be good. Do your homework and make informed decisions.

We had an election just before I wrote this chapter. On the ballot was a multi-billion dollar state transportation tax referendum. In return for paying an extra 1 percent sales tax for a decade, a large variety of projects would be funded for our area roads and transportation infrastructure. The referendum failed by a large margin. Ironically, both those on the left and right voted against it, albeit for different reasons. The common thread seemed to be that nobody trusted the government to do what it promised.

From my view, the referendum was set up in a way that allowed flawed arguments to be made by all sides. There were some very much needed road projects on the funding list. However, the huge sums of money targeted for rail and other mass transit projects were viewed as wasteful by many on the right. Proponents of the referendum stressed how we'd be voting against the needed roadwork if we voted against the referendum. That is true in the absolute sense. However, those on the right questioned the premise that to get the needed roadwork accomplished, we had to fund huge, unrelated public transit projects as well. Why did it need to be all or nothing?

Those on the left voted against the referendum because it didn't include funding for even more rail and mass transit. They didn't see why they should fund what they viewed as unnecessary road projects to finance the transit projects. Those on the left voted against the referendum for the exact opposite reason that those on the right voted against it. The left didn't want the road projects and the right didn't want the transit projects. Both sides voted against the bill, but they agreed with opposite parts of it!

Both sides agreed there was too much waste. It just happened that what they viewed as waste was the other side's priorities! This is an example where people took a stand and voted against something that had some items that would have been good by their own standards. However, they wanted to send the message that only a limited amount of waste is acceptable. In that concept, at least the majority agreed. It took an effort to understand the arguments being made and how they would be resolved. Without the effort to be an educated voter, it would have been very easy to vote against what you thought you were voting for.

Taking Action

- Will you make a commitment to take your right to vote very seriously and to exercise it every chance you get?

- Will you make it a priority to be an educated voter and to research the issues and candidates and make informed choices? Don't vote based on sound bites alone.

- Have you thought about how you feel about many important issues? If not, get started today. It is important for you to form an educated opinion.

- Once you know what you stand for, it will take effort to identify the candidates, parties, and organizations that generally agree with your views. Nobody will ever match you 100 percent, so you may have to vary your voting pattern, depending on the options presented.

- Research the arguments and opinions from all sides of an issue. It will help you solidify your position and you'll learn a lot, too.

About the Author

Bill Franks is the Chief Analytics Officer at the International Institute for Analytics (IIA). In this role, he helps guide IIA's global community of analytics practitioners in determining the best strategy for their particular analytics needs. He provides perspective on trends in analytics and big data, and helps clients understand how IIA can support their efforts to improve analytic performance.

Bill serves on the advisory boards of multiple university and professional analytics programs and has previously held a range of executive positions in analytics, including several years as Chief Analytics Officer for Teradata (NYSE: TDC). He is also an active speaker and has presented at dozens of events over the past few years.

He earned a Master's degree in Applied Statistics from North Carolina State University and a Bachelor's degree in Applied Statistics from Virginia Tech.

Bill's previous books include *Taming The Big Data Tidal Wave* (John Wiley & Sons) where he applied two decades of experience working with clients on large-scale analytics initiatives to outline what it takes to succeed in today's world of big data and analytics. His second book, *The Analytics Revolution* (John Wiley & Sons), lays out how to move beyond using analytics to find important insights in data (large and small) and into operationalizing those insights at scale to truly impact a business. His blog, Analytics Matters, addresses the transformation required to make analytics a core component of business decisions.

I Need To Tell You Something: Life lessons from a father for his teenage children was written from Bill's perspective as a businessman and a parent. As a father, he is also a leader, advisor, and teacher. His passion for both roles brings him to share life lessons not only with his own children, but with other families as well.

CPSIA information can be obtained
at www.ICGtesting.com
Printed in the USA
FFOW04n0934111017
40954FF